Elena Vilar

Woven Art

*15 modern weaving projects
for you and your home*

SEARCH PRESS

CONTENTS

WHY WEAVE? 5

BEFORE YOU BEGIN 6

BASIC TOOLS AND MATERIALS 8

CHOOSING A LOOM 10

THE WARP THREADS 12

THE CHOICE OF FIBRES 14

MAKING VEGETABLE DYE 16

HANDMADE T-SHIRT YARN 18

OTHER TOOLS AND ACCESSORIES 20

POMPOMS AND TASSELS 22

MAKING A CARDBOARD LOOM 24

MAKING A WOODEN LOOM 26

WARPING A RECTANGULAR LOOM 28

WARPING A CIRCULAR LOOM 30

A BIT OF TECHNIQUE 32

THE WEAVES 34

First steps 36

36 BASIC WEAVING

46 DIAGONAL CLOUD WEAVE

58 WEAVING SHAPES

Simple weaves 68

68 BRAIDED (SOUMAK) WEAVES

80 FRINGED WEAVES

88 EMBROIDERED WEAVES

WEAVING USING BARK 92

CIRCULAR WEAVING 100

WEAVING WITHOUT A LOOM 108

More ambitious projects
128

MACRAMÉ CLOUD WEAVE 116

HANGING VASE 128

WOVEN NECKLACE 132

WOVEN DREAM-CATCHER 136

WOVEN CLUTCH BAG 146

BERBER-INSPIRED RUG 152

AUTHOR'S THANKS AND PUBLICATION DETAILS 160

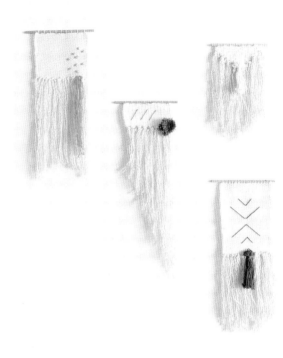
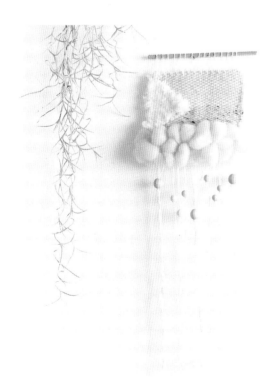

Why weave ?

Weaving has been a big part of my life. I had already been surrounded by it as a child, as both my mother and great-grandmother were established weavers, but it was only a little over three years ago that I embarked on weaving more seriously, in the more contemporary style seen in recent years.

I weave almost every day; it is almost a craving. The act of weaving both relaxes and invigorates me. It creates a tranquil bubble, a place where I can let my hands take control and where I am forced to concentrate and do only one thing at a time. Weaving is repetitive but free, and its wide variety of techniques make it wonderfully unpredictable and allow you to create truly unique designs – you can use existing methods, or invent ones to achieve the effect you want. For me it has become a means of expression, like painting, sculpture, music or photography. There is plenty of scope for your imagination to run wild.

Weaving is an ancestral art that has stood the test of centuries, alternating between utilitarian and decorative uses: from a small piece of simple fabric used in the home, through to lavish tapestries depicting scenes from literature. Many of us have been unaware of how it has been a basis and inspiration for a multitude of everyday objects in the modern world.

The present decade has seen the revival of this 1000-year-old craft in interior design, as a result of its warm, decorative, handmade qualities. Today, weaves are often used as wall hangings, their functional side having given way to a more aesthetic role. A picture formed of wool, sometimes graphic, sometimes abstract, in a range of colours and textures... Woven art.

If you are a beginner to this ancient craft, use this book to learn the basic techniques and discover the key to inventing your own special style of weaving. There are fifteen projects, each focusing on different methods that will help you get to grips with this craft and give free rein to your creativity. I urge you not to try to produce identical pieces of weaving to those shown in this book (although, of course, you can if you want to), but rather use them as inspiration to try and establish your own creations. The variety of techniques covered inside are more than enough to get you started on your own projects.

Give it a go, make mistakes, start again – just have fun! You'll discover weaving is addictive, and with multiple techniques come endless possibilities.

Elena

BEFORE YOU BEGIN

BASIC TOOLS AND MATERIALS

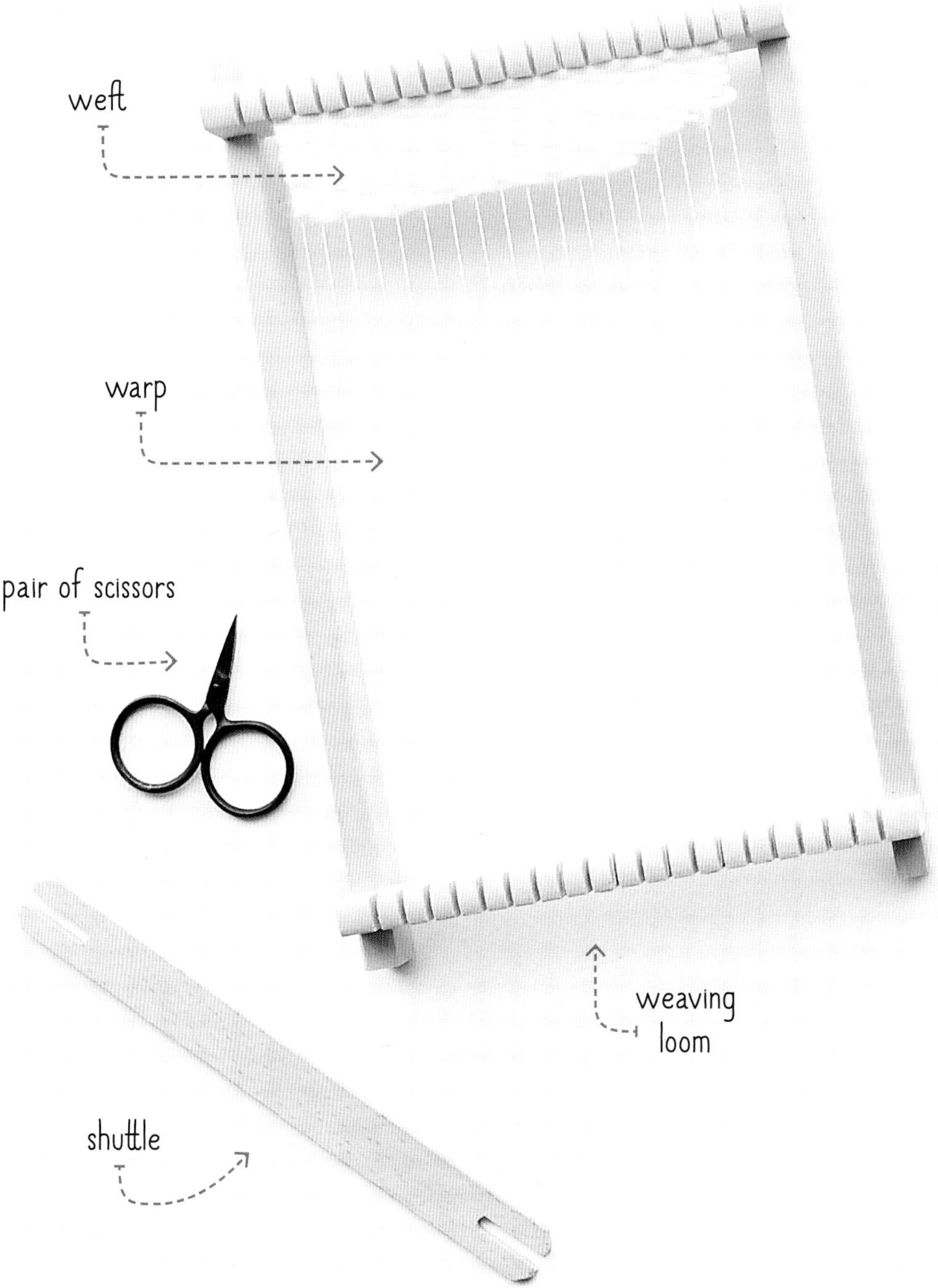

weft

warp

pair of scissors

weaving loom

shuttle

8

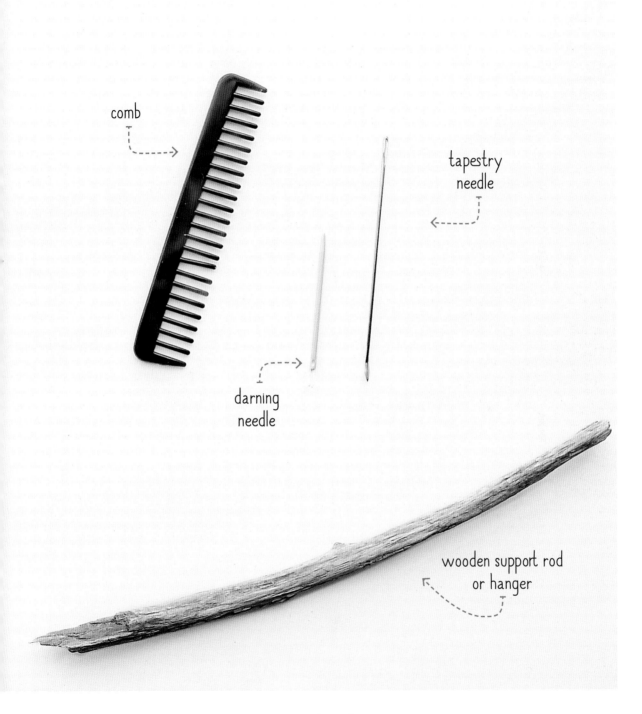

comb

tapestry
needle

darning
needle

wooden support rod
or hanger

CHOOSING A LOOM

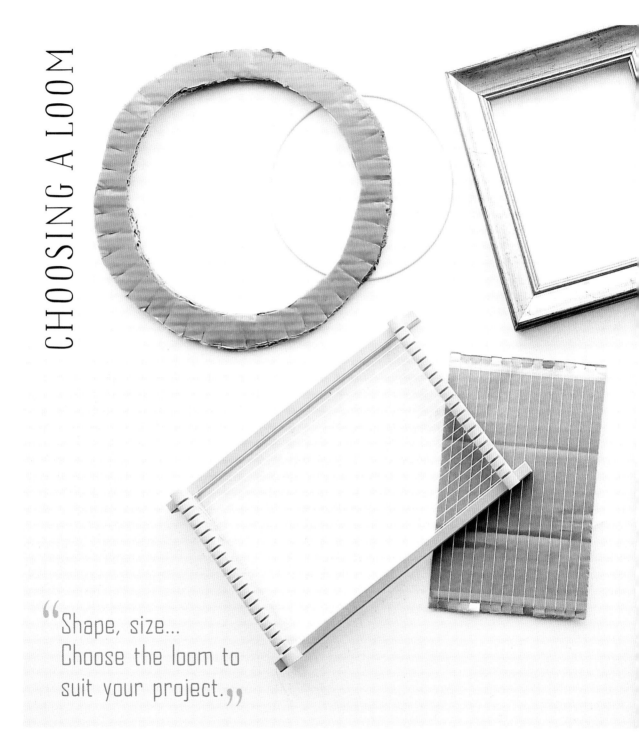

"Shape, size...
Choose the loom to
suit your project."

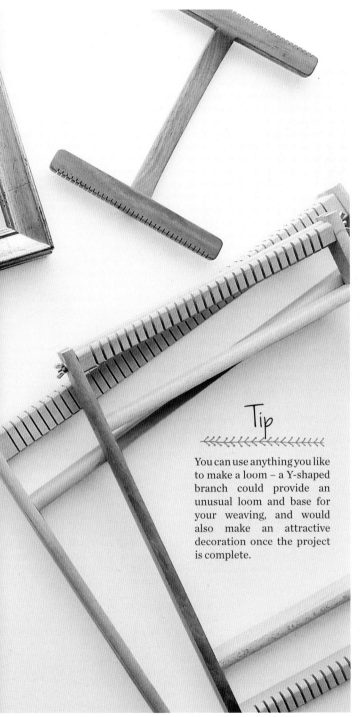

In this book, we will use mostly rectangular weaving looms. These are cheap, easy to use and offer multiple possibilities for expressing yourself!

There is no need to buy any expensive equipment when you begin to give weaving a go. When you first start out, you can use a cardboard loom (see page 24) or a simple picture frame on to which you hammer a few nails (see page 27).

For future projects you can decide whether you want to upgrade or downsize your loom for the design you require. Some looms also have a rigid or rotating heddle. The heddle is a sort of rigid bar, its shape differing slightly depending on the type, which allows you to raise and lower the warp threads quickly. This makes weaving easier, especially if the design is large. The warp threads on a professional loom are prepared in the same way as on a handmade loom, although a heddled loom will be threaded slightly differently, depending on the type. Personally, I do not use heddled looms very much.

Use a rectangular or circular loom, depending on the shape of the piece you want to make. Whatever the shape or size of your loom, the process remains the same; you will just notice some differences in how you handle them. Smaller looms are easily transportable, and it is always nice to have a thin, flat loom to slide into your bag when travelling.

It is not always easy to find the perfect loom. You may find you will need to test several, because what suits one person might not suit another. It is often a question of personal taste, comfort and handling. Try out different ones, have fun, get used to the different shapes of looms and you will soon find the one that works for you. It is also possible, with a bit of DIY, to make yourself the perfect loom that fits your own specifications.

Tip

You can use anything you like to make a loom – a Y-shaped branch could provide an unusual loom and base for your weaving, and would also make an attractive decoration once the project is complete.

THE WARP THREADS

Coloured threads

A black or coloured warp thread will add
a discreet touch of colour to your weave.
If you want it to show, don't push the weft
threads too closely together.

The warp threads form the backbone of your weave and are the foundations around which the weft is woven.

To give your project a unique quality, use different coloured bands of warp threads

From neutrals to bright colours, the choice of threads is very wide! You can use any type of fibre to form the warp. Cotton or woollen yarn, hemp or linen twine, string, and even strips of material. Anything is possible, but there is just one constraint: the strength of the yarn. The yarn must be able to take the tension of the weave without breaking, otherwise your work might come apart before your eyes – especially if you do not manage to secure the broken ends in time...

SECURING A BROKEN WARP THREAD

What if, despite your precautions, the warp thread breaks when you are mid-project? Take a short length of matching yarn and knot it to the broken ends, and then pull the two knotted lengths tightly. Continue with your weaving. Once the project is complete, the knots will be completely hidden.

TWO TIPS FOR CREATING SIMPLE FRINGES

One easy way to make fringes for your design is to leave the ends of the warp threads hanging, once you have knotted them up against the bottom of your weave. This method will leave you with short but effective fringing (see page 92 for an example similar to this). Alternatively, you can add fine fringing using the same yarn used for the warp thread, to make them look like an extension of the weave (see also pages 53 and 54).

THE CHOICE OF FIBRES

The fibres are the most important constituent of a weaving project. They are what give your design body and shape. There are numerous different types, both natural and synthetic. Some consideration may be needed on which fibre will work best for your weaving depending on how you intend to use or display your weave.

NATURAL FIBRES

Below are some examples of natural fibres I often use for my own designs. Some give weaves a particular smell. I love the feel and smell of a natural weave!

Vegetable fibres:	Animal fibres:
manila hemp	alpaca
hemp	angora
cotton	cashmere
jute	wool
linen	mohair
raffia...	silk...

SYNTHETIC FIBRES

Synthetic fibres offer an infinite array of colours, looks and texture, and provide plenty of scope for eccentricity. They can be more durable than natural fibres, have greater stretch and are less prone to damage from stains or the sun. However, some synthetic fibres are vulnerable to hot temperatures and may not respond well to hot washing.

UPCYCLED FIBRES

Weaving provides a great opportunity to recycle old clothes or curtains, simply by cutting them into strips (see page 18 for more information on how to do this). You can also hunt for balls of yarn in second-hand (thrift/op) shops, or dye fibres to give them a more personal (and sometimes unpredictable) look.

MAKING VEGETABLE DYE

"Avocado skin gives an attractive pink shade."

"Onion skins result in a soft yellow."

"Rosemary dyes a delicate yellow-brown."

Dyeing material or wool yourself means you can create your own colours that are unique to your woven design.

Of course, there are multiple dyes on the market in a wide range of colours, but it can be very satisfying to colour the fibres yourself and see the beautiful – and often surprising – results of using natural products such as vegetables, fruit and leaves.

TOOLS

You will need an enamel or stainless-steel pot and a wooden spatula.
Warning: Keep these dyeing pots just for this purpose; once they have been used for dyeing, their cooking days are over.

FOR A LASTING COLOUR

To make a new shade permanent, you need to use a solution known as a **mordant** to bind in the colour. There are different mordants available, but the easiest to use is **alum** which is used at a ratio of 10 per cent to the weight of the fibre. For example, for 100 grams (3½oz) of fibre, use 10 grams (2 teaspoons) of alum.

METHOD

1 Rinse the fibres and set to one side. Fill the pot with water, heat it gently on a hob until lukewarm and then add the mordant. Once the mordant has dissolved, add the damp fibres to the pot and allow them to simmer, stirring regularly for at least 45 minutes. Set the fibres aside once more.

2 Boil the natural products (onion skin, rosemary, avocado skin, etc.) in the solution for a good hour, until the water has taken the colour. Pass the solution through a sieve to remove all solid vegetable matter, then pour it back into the pot and add the fibres. Simmer again until they have achieved the desired shade.

3 Remove the pot from the heat and allow to cool. Rinse the fibres repeatedly until the water runs clear. Then, simply leave to dry.

HANDMADE T-SHIRT YARN

Weaving is a good way of recycling. Rather than throwing away your old T-shirts, save money on fibres by turning them into yarn! You could collect your friends' unused clothes too.

1 Fold a T-shirt lengthways. You want it almost, but not completely, folded in half – fold the fabric so that the edge of the right side of the T-shirt lies about 3cm (1¼in) shorter than the left side of the T-shirt underneath.

2 Cut off the top part of the T-shirt, under the sleeves.

3 Cut off the hem. Start cutting a strip around 1cm (½in) wide from the fold line along the long side of the T-shirt. Stop before you reach the edge of the underneath layer.

4 Repeat Step 3 along the full length of the T-shirt. It does not matter if the strips are not all the same width.

18

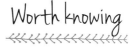

6 Continue to cut, linking the cuts diagonally.

5 Open out the T-shirt in front of you with the non-cut edge going down the middle. This will give you something that looks like a rib cage. Cut the first strip off diagonally, from the central seam.

Worth knowing

If you make sure your first cut is on the diagonal, your subsequent cuts will automatically be in a parallel direction.

7 You can generally cut the whole thing into one long strip. Stretch the strip so it curls in on itself.

8 Roll the T-shirt yarn into a ball. It is ready to be woven.

Tip

If you make a mistake, do not throw the strips away: simply knot them together to make a long piece of T-shirt yarn. You can still use it, and you can try again next time. You can make balls of denim and plenty of other materials in the same way.

OTHER TOOLS AND ACCESSORIES

feathers

bark

crochet hook

wooden or pearl beads

wooden rod

strips of material or faux leather

dried flowers

20

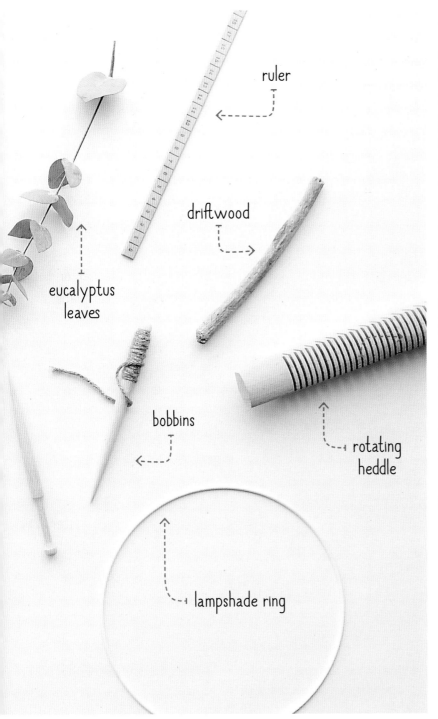

ruler

driftwood

eucalyptus
leaves

bobbins

rotating
heddle

lampshade ring

You need very little equipment for weaving, but there are always additional tools you can use to make the process easier. There are also a few accessories you can incorporate into your weave which will enhance and add an imaginative touch to your woven designs.

EXTRA TOOLS TO SPEED THINGS UP

These include a rotating heddle, to lift every other warp thread while you thread the weft; a crochet hook, to catch hold of a thread or attach a pompom; lampshade rings, to stiffen the edges and keep a circular weave nice and round; wooden bobbins, to help you change fibres more easily on smaller surfaces; and a wooden ruler or rod inserted between the warp threads, used as an alternative rotating heddle or to hang your weaving at the end.

EMBELLISHMENTS TO ENHANCE

Consider adding some non-woollen, non-yarn features to your weaving: bark or dried flowers, beads, copper pipe, pieces of pottery, faux leather, scraps of material, some gold leaf or paper laid directly on the weave, to name a few.

POMPOMS AND TASSELS

EQUIPMENT

1 ball of wool
1 pair of scissors
1 comb, fork or piece
of cardboard

Making pompoms

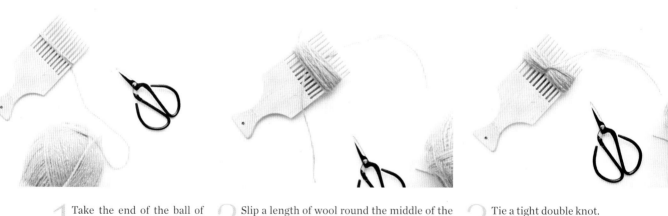

1 Take the end of the ball of wool and wind it round the comb several times.

2 Slip a length of wool round the middle of the wrapped wool, passing it up through the teeth of the comb.

3 Tie a tight double knot.

Tip

The more wool you wind round, the thicker the pompom will be.

4 Slide the tied wool off the comb and snip the loops at both ends.

5 You can trim the pompom to the shape and look you desire.

Making tassels

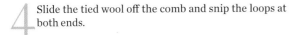

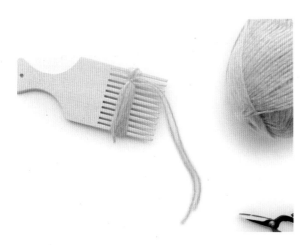

1 Start off in the same way as the pompom, but this time tie the length of wool further to one side of the the comb.

2 Slide the tied wool off the comb and snip through one loop, along the longer bottom end.

MAKING A CARDBOARD LOOM

EQUIPMENT FOR MAKING A RECTANGULAR LOOM

1 large piece of cardboard
1 pair of scissors or craft knife
1 roll of duct tape
1 pencil
1 ruler

EQUIPMENT FOR MAKING A CIRCULAR LOOM

1 large piece of cardboard
1 pair of scissors
1 fine-tipped marker pen
1 roll of sticky tape or tube of glue

Making a rectangular loom

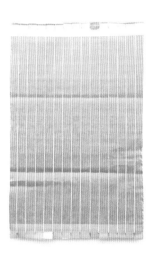

1 Cut a rectangle from the cardboard to the size that you require. The loom in the photo is 23 x 15cm (9 x 6in).

2 Apply duct tape along the short edges to strengthen them, so that the cardboard doesn't fold under the tension of the warp threads.

3 Using a pencil, mark off every 1cm (½in) along the top and bottom edges of the loom. Cut a notch at each mark with the scissors or craft knife. The notches along the top should line up with the ones along the bottom.

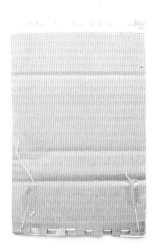

It is easier if...

... you make an even number of notches. This makes it simpler to knot the warp threads in pairs when you have finished weaving. Use duct tape to hold the ends of the warp threads in place on the back of the loom.

Making a circular loom

1 Cut two identical circles from fairly thick cardboard and cut out the middles, leaving you with two rings approx. 3cm (1¼in) thick. In the photo, the exterior diameter is approx. 29cm (11½in) and the cut-away circle approx. 26cm (10¼in) in diameter.

2 On one of the cardboard rings, use the pen to mark where the notches will be. There are forty-three marks on this loom.

Tip

For circular weaving, you need an odd number of notches so that the alternate over–under weaving pattern is created automatically – i.e. having gone round once ('under– over') with the yarn, where the next round begins the weaving will automatically start with the opposite pattern ('over–under').

3 Stick the two cardboard rings securely together with sticky tape or glue so they cannot move. This ensures the loom does not fold under the tension of the warp threads while you are weaving.

4 With scissors, cut the notches around the edge of the cardboard rings, making sure that you do not cut right the way through to the centre.

MAKING A WOODEN LOOM

A wooden loom requires a few more tools than a cardboard loom, but it will provide you with the solidity needed for much larger weaving projects. As before with the cardboard looms, you can make a wooden loom to whatever size you choose.

TOOLS

4 sticks of wood
1 saw
1 pencil
pack of nails
4 small brackets
16 screws
1 screwdriver
1 hammer
1 ruler

1 Saw the sticks of wood to your required lengths. Place them end to end to make a frame, and then nail the corners together to hold them in place. Put a bracket in each corner, then screw into place. This will strengthen the corners so they do not move under the tension of the threads.

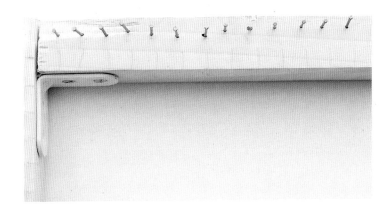

2 Using a ruler and pencil, mark off every 1cm (½in) along the two opposite sides of the frame. Hammer in a nail at each marker. Leave the nails sticking out by at least 1cm (½in).

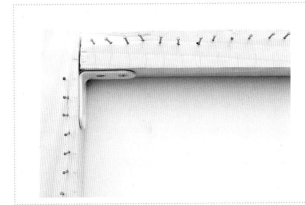

Two looms in one

You could also put nails along all four sides so you will have two looms in one: one if you weave lengthways, producing a portrait-style weave, and another if you weave widthways to make a weave with a landscape format. Simply turn it round depending on the shape you want your project to take.

3 To warp your loom pass the yarn around two nails at the top and the opposite two at the bottom. Repeat along the full width of the loom. There is more information on warping a loom on pages 28–31.

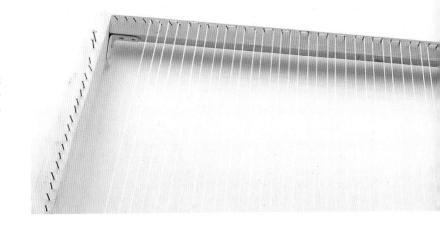

WARPING A RECTANGULAR LOOM

Now you have a loom, you need to string the warp – the vertical threads that act as the foundation for all weaving. Using either of the following methods, you can make your weft tighter or looser as you please.

Simple warping method

  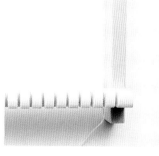

1 Lay the loom flat in front of you.

2 Make a square (reef) knot around the first notch at the bottom. Pull tight.

3 Bring the thread up to the opposite notch, at the top of the loom.

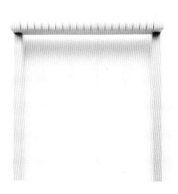 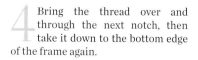 

4 Bring the thread over and through the next notch, then take it down to the bottom edge of the frame again.

5 Pass the thread through the notch at the opposite end, bring it round and up though the next notch, and so on. The threads should be parallel.

6 Continue in the same way across the full width of the loom. Finish by double knotting the end of the yarn at the bottom of the frame.

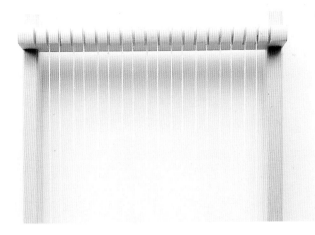

Tip

ᐊᐊᐊᐊᐊᐊᐊᐊᐊᐊᐊᐊᐊᐊ

You can attach the ends of the warp threads to either end of the loom, but ideally they should be tied off on the same side, either at the top or at the bottom. This will guarantee an even number of warp threads: using even threads makes weaving easier, and you can knot the warp threads together in pairs once you have finished weaving.

Double warping method ....

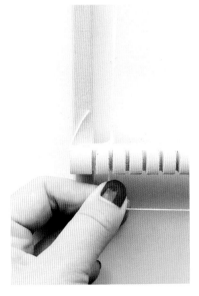

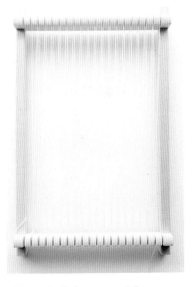

1 Start as you would for a single warp, following Steps 1–4.

2 Instead of putting the thread round the next notch, put it back through the first notch so you have two threads per notch at both top and bottom.

This method gives you a tighter, more accurate weft; this is ideal if your project contains lots of patterns.

WARPING A CIRCULAR LOOM

1 Lay the loom flat in front of you. On this one, there are forty-three notches.

2 Knot the yarn around one of the notches in the frame. It does not matter where you start.

3 Pull the thread tightly across to the opposite notch. You have effectively divided the loom in half: there should now be twenty empty notches above and twenty-one empty notches below.

4 Pass the thread round the notch to the right, then take it across to the other side and wrap it around the notch to the right of the threaded notch there. The threads should cross in the centre.

5 Continue in the same way right round the circumference of the loom, wrapping the thread around the notch to the right and taking it across to the other side.

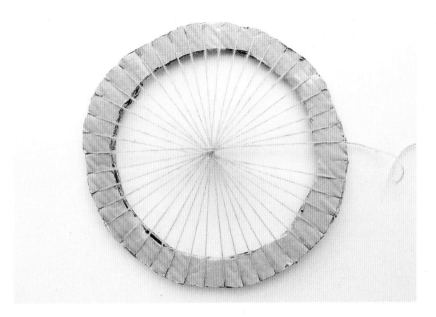

6 When you reach the last notch, you should find yourself without an empty notch on the opposite side. This is correct! The odd number of notches means the weft rows will alternate naturally.

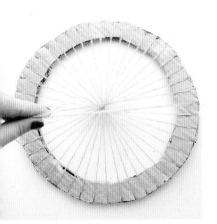

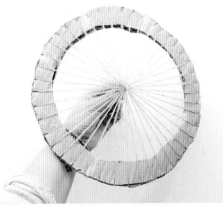

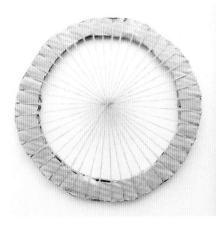

Now it's time to start weaving!

7 Bring the end of the thread towards the middle of the weave and knot it in the centre, at the spot where all the warp threads cross. Cut away the remaining thread.

31

A BIT OF TECHNIQUE

Now that your loom is ready, no doubt you are wondering how to use it and what to do with all the tails of yarn hanging out. Here are a few answers.

WHICH DIRECTION TO WEAVE IN?

First of all, work out how you would like to hold your loom: small looms sit nicely on the table or in your lap, while larger ones can be propped vertically against a wall or held in place with supports attached to the loom – simple struts of wood on the side can do this.

Horizontal or vertical? Generally, you start to weave your yarn on to the loom from the bottom up, working upwards from where the fringe will be and towards where the support rod will go. It is then easier to ensure the rows of woven yarn sit snugly against each other, pushing them downwards as you go.

Personally, I always start my weaving at the top where the rod will be and then work my way down towards the fringe. I often turn the loom upside down to make certain stitches, such as rya knots (see page 42) and 'knotted' rya knots (see page 54) , easier to create. When this is the case, my weaving goes from top to bottom. I always leave the fringes until last, rather than starting with them; I find it easier to envisage the project design if I begin at the top. However, this is a personal preference and others may wish to do the opposite.

It is up to you which method you choose. Try out the different options; you will probably find your favourite will emerge naturally as one method will simply feel more comfortable and easier to work with. No doubt you will find your own way of weaving. At the end of the day, it doesn't matter how you weave – it is the final result that counts.

WHEN TO WORK IN TAILS OF YARN

When you change the yarn at the beginning and ends of rows, you will leave tails hanging from the sides. This is not a problem; you just need to work them in when you have finished weaving. Instructions on how to do this will follow later.

Some people enjoy applying these finishing touches but others find it boring. I am one of the latter – it is not my favourite part of the process at all! If you feel the same, you can just work the tails in between completed rows as you go. This creates a much neater finish, and also you will not have left the most boring bit until last.

THE WEAVES

First steps 36

Simple weaves 68

More ambitious projects 116

BASIC WEAVING

This project is ideal for mastering the art of creating simple weaves using the basic stitch and fringing. These two processes will be all you need for many of your ideas. In this section you will learn also how to change yarn, work in the ends and attach your weave to a support rod.

TOOLS

1 cardboard loom
1 tapestry needle
1 darning needle
1 pair of fabric scissors
1 piece of driftwood
1 comb

FIBRES

1 reel of white cotton twine
1 ball of black metallic wool
1 ball of black speckled wool
1 ball of grey metallic wool
1 ball of fluorescent-yellow cotton yarn
1 skein of ecru merino roving
1 ball of white wool

STITCHES USED

basic stitch
rya knot

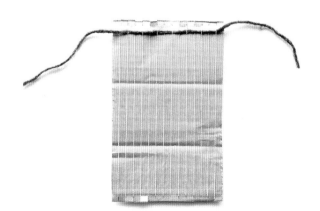

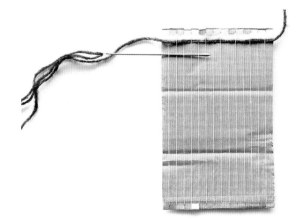

1 To start with, thread a tapestry needle with the black metallic wool. Pass the needle under and over the warp threads across the whole width of the loom – I have worked from right to left. Leave a starting 'tail', or length of wool, around 5cm (2in) long hanging to the side of the loom where you have begun the row. This tail will be worked in when you have finished weaving.

2 Once you have finished the first row, turn the needle round and weave a row underneath, this time in a pattern opposite to the one before: if the yarn went over the warp thread at the end of the previous row, begin the next row by going under it. Likewise, if the thread went under it, this time go over the top. Weave back across to where you started.

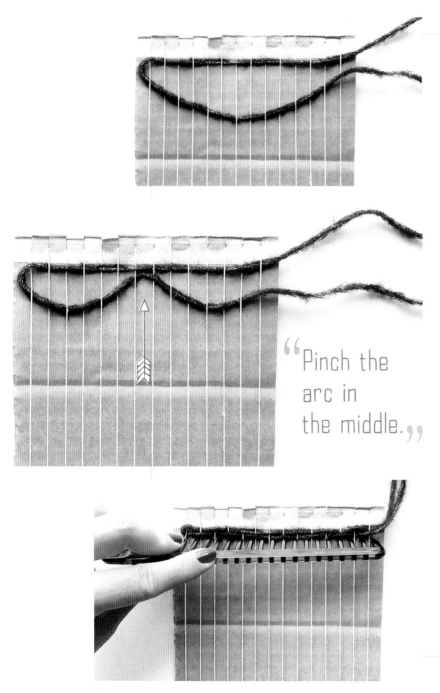

How to keep the weft tension the same

It is easy to inadvertently pull the weft thread tighter and tighter as you work; this will result in a weave that gradually narrows in width. Here is a technique for keeping the same tension throughout the whole weave.

When you begin a row, weave the wool in loosely in the shape of an arc (see top picture). Pinch the arc in the middle with your index finger and thumb (see middle picture), and then press the whole row up using a comb to make sure the rows are nice and close together (see bottom picture). This approach will prevent your weaving from getting too tight, and it ensures that the tension is maintained throughout.

That being said, a project that gets narrower or has wonky edges might be just the look you are after! Personally, I love the organic, free-form effect that these small differences in technique can provide.

"Pinch the arc in the middle."

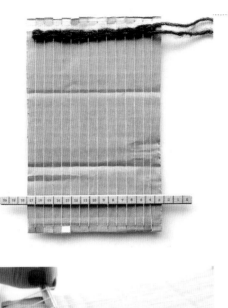

The easiest way to weave the needle

Inserting a strip of wood – known formally as a 'shed stick', 'weaving sword' or 'shuttle' – over and under the warp threads, following the pattern of the stitch row you are working on, makes it much easier to pull the weft thread through. When you lift the shed stick, every other warp thread (the odd numbers in the photo) will be lifted together at once, forming what is called the 'shed' through which the yarn and needle can easily pass. As you can see, a basic ruler makes an effective alternative to a specially-designed shuttle!

> Every other warp thread is raised.

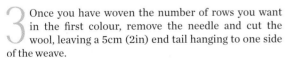

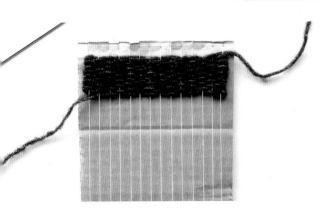

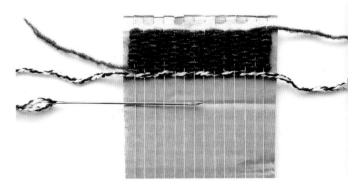

3 Once you have woven the number of rows you want in the first colour, remove the needle and cut the wool, leaving a 5cm (2in) end tail hanging to one side of the weave.

4 Changing the wool when starting a new row is very easy. You simply need to choose a new colour (in the photo I have picked speckled black wool), then begin to weave in the basic stitch as before, ensuring you are working opposite to the row above and that a 5cm (2in) tail of yarn is left at the start. Continue until you have completed the desired number of rows.

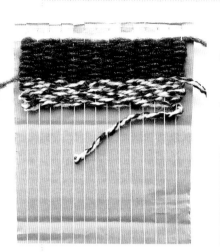

Invisible join

Sometimes, a length of yarn may not be quite long enough. To make an invisible join, leave a 3cm (1¼in) tail of your remaining yarn hanging at the back of your weave, under the warp threads. Take another length of the same colour, insert it over and under the warp threads – corresponding with the weft pattern of the unfinished row – and then cross this new tail over the old one. Do not knot them together. Push the rows snugly together with your fingers or a comb. You will not be able to see the join. You can also use this method to change colour in the middle of a row.

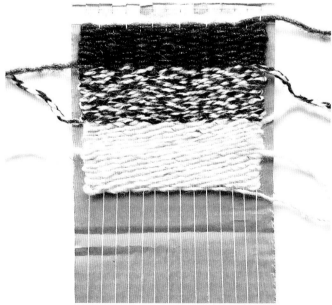

"The tails will be worked in at the end."

5 When you feel that your second band of colour is large enough, weave a third band (here in light grey) in the same way. In this photo, you can see that the join in the speckled wool is totally invisible once the rows have been pushed together. Leave the beginning and end tails of yarn hanging for now. They will be worked in at the end to create a neat, attractive finish.

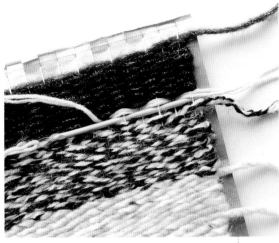

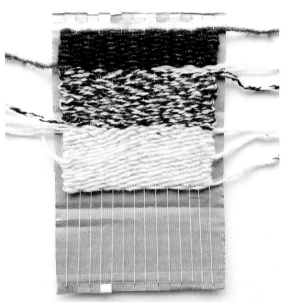

Adding rows

If you are not so keen on the final look of your weave, or if there are any gaps on the edge which you would like to fill, extra rows can easily be added and will introduce an interesting touch of colour to your weave too.

Using your fingers, gently push apart the rows where you wish to add the new colour. Using a needle (I have used a darning needle), weave in the new yarn, ensuring that you are following the weft pattern in the working row. Weave an even number of rows to ensure the over–under pattern is respected. Here, the fluorescent cotton is not as thick as the other yarns so I have used it double on the needle for balance.

6 Cut some lengths of ecru merino roving, all the same size. You will use these to make the fringing. Note that the fringing is made by folding these lengths in half, so decide how long you would like your finished fringes to and then double this length for cutting.

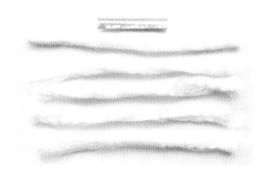

7 You are going to make the fringing using the simple rya knot technique.

As the merino roving is very thick, the rya knot is formed around four warp threads, divided into two lots of two. Lay the length of wool across the first four warp threads. Pass the left end under the two warp threads on the left-hand side, and the right end under the two warp threads on the right-hand side. Bring both ends up through the centre. The wool is now wound around two warp threads on each side, from the outside in.

Gently pull the ends downwards to tighten the knot.

8 Continue to form rya knots across the full width of the weave.

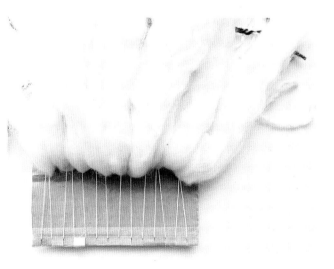

Tip

Once it is completed, lay the ends of each finished rya knot upwards towards the top of weave. This keeps them out of your way and stops them from getting tatty while you continue to work.

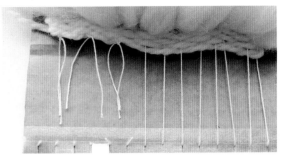

10 Cut the warp threads two by two at the bottom of the loom, then tie them together tightly with a double knot, right up against the weave. Make sure you keep the tension of the weave the same throughout, otherwise the weave will not be straight.

To ensure even tension

Try knotting the warp threads alternately, starting on the far-left and -right sides and then working your way in. The last knot should be in the middle of the weave. This will keep the tension consistent across the weaving.

9 To hold the rya knot fringes in place and secure the rest of the weaving, work a few rows of basic stitch in a corresponding colour yarn. Push the rows snugly together with your fingers or a comb. The weaving part is now complete.

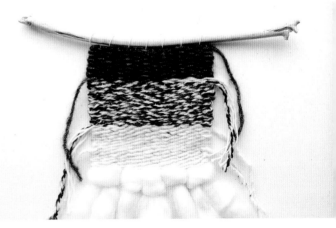

11 Carefully lift the weave off the top of the frame and pass a piece of driftwood through the loops at the top. To keep the two together as securely as possible, gently slide the support rod through the loops in a direction contrary to the pattern woven on the first row.

12 Carefully push the weave up against the support rod so that it does not come undone.

"Here is the back of the weave before you work in the tails of yarn."

"The yarn tails have been worked in for an attractive finish."

13 Turn the weave over and work in the hanging tails using a darning needle. Thread the needle with one of the tails, pass it vertically through the rows until you meet the end of the same colour band, and then cut off the remaining piece of wool flat against the back. Repeat.

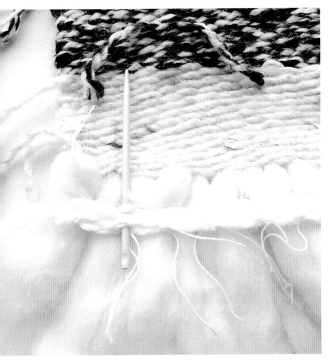

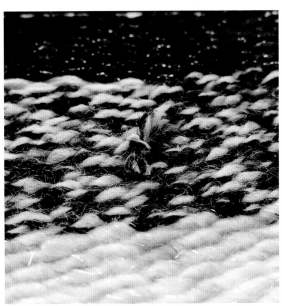

14 Weave in the warp threads in the same way. Cut off any strands that are still showing.

15 For any tails of yarn in the middle (such as joined yarn, see page 40) you can simply knot them and cut off the excess to the knot. If you want the tails to be invisible, thread them on to a darning needle and then carefully pull both vertically through several rows before cutting off the excess flat against the weave.

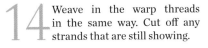

DIAGONAL CLOUD WEAVE

As in knitting or crochet, it is possible to make rows shorter or longer in a weave. Known as increasing or decreasing this technique is very easy to master and will enable you to form lots of different shapes of varying complexity. This project also gives you the opportunity to learn another kind of rya knot and a way of creating a cloud-like texture with your woven yarn.

TOOLS

1 weaving loom
1 tapestry needle
1 darning needle
1 pair of scissors
1 support rod
1 comb

FIBRES

1 reel of black cotton twine
1 ball of purple wool
1 ball of pale pink wool
1 ball of gold wool
1 skein of ecru merino roving
1 ball of white wool

STITCHES USED

basic stitch
decreasing and increasing
'knotted' rya knot
cloud texture effect
hem stitch

1 Leaving a tail of 5cm (2in) and starting the weave from the right-hand side, pass the purple wool over and under the warp threads to the other side. Take it back again, under and over the warp threads, to create the second row.

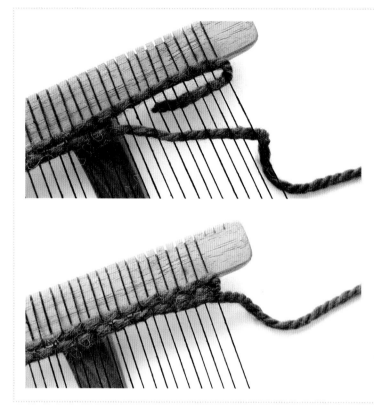

Achieving a perfect weave

It can be satisfying to create a tidy weave, with no tails hanging from the sides to be worked in later.

To do this, weave a little of the 5cm (2in) beginning tail of wool between two woven rows (see top-left image) and leave the remaining end hanging at the back. Push the rows together tightly using your fingers or a comb (see bottom-left image). Snip off the remaining wool at the back so it sits flush with the back of the weave.

If you are using very flexible or fine yarn, the woven-in tail will be barely visible. However, with thicker fibres, such as T-shirt yarn or cord, it will show through slightly; this is not necessarily a bad thing.

We are going to use this method on this project. On future projects you can decide what suits you the best.

2 In the third row work a basic stitch almost to the very end; when you reach the last warp thread, ignore it and weave back in the opposite direction to form the fourth row. Ensure that you weave in a pattern contrary to the previous row. Push the rows together carefully with your fingers or a comb. You have just completed your first decrease. Continue to reduce the rows in this way, omitting an additional warp thread with each row. You will gradually see a diagonal shape emerge.

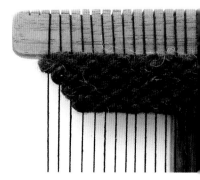

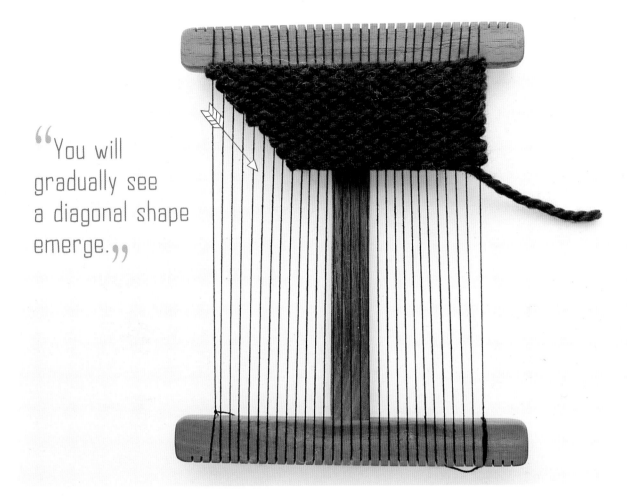

"You will gradually see a diagonal shape emerge."

3 When you reach the end of your band of colour, leave a 5cm (2in) tail of wool. This time, work it in immediately by weaving it between the two last rows and leaving the remaining length of wool hanging at the back. Carefully push the rows together to conceal the woven-in tail. Turn the frame around and cut off the end of the yarn so that it sits flush against the back of the weave.

Finished purple diagonal.

4 Change to the pale pink wool and start weaving from the right-hand side of the loom once again, up to the end of the purple line of wool.

Tip

If you are using a finer yarn, you can double it to even out the thickness.

5 To increase the band of pink wool, forming a diagonal shape in the opposite direction, increase the width of the weave by gradually weaving in an additional warp thread with each new row.

6 Once you have completed the diagonal, work in the tail end of the wool between the last two rows and then push the rows snugly together with a comb to ensure that it cannot be seen. You should now have an empty triangle shape that you are going to fill with the gold wool.

Leaving an empty space

You may choose not to fill in the empty space on the left; with certain weaves, this can create a very attractive effect.

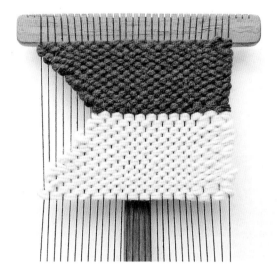

7 To fill in the shape, thread a darning needle with a length of gold wool. Start by going twice round the first warp thread, to work the necessary stitches for the first and second rows, then continue to weave as normal, following the basic stitch pattern. With each row, work as far as you can until you meet the purple yarn woven earlier, and then turn around and go back in the opposite direction to form the subsequent row. You will need to gradually increase the rows and then decrease them once again, when you meet the pink band of colour, to complete your gold triangle.

As you work, make sure you don't pull the wool too tight; this gives it a bit of body.

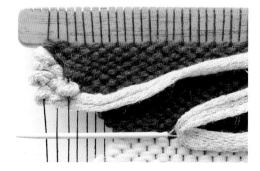

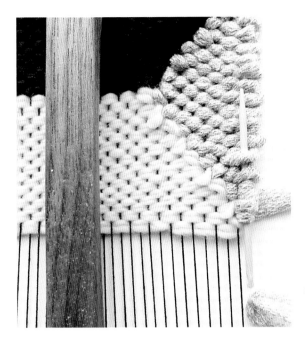

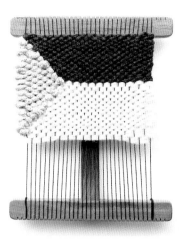

8 Turn the loom over and work the ends of the gold wool into the back of the weave by pulling the tails up through the rows vertically with a darning needle. Cut off the excess wool flush against the weave. You have now finished the final triangle.

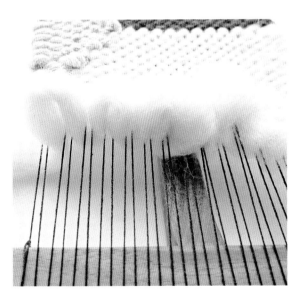

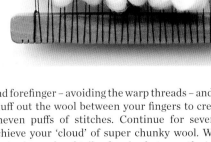

9 To create the cloud effect, take a relatively long length of ecru merino roving and weave it through using the basic stitch. As roving wool is very thick, go over and under two warp threads at a time. To create the 'clouds', pinch the loop of super chunky wool between your thumb and forefinger – avoiding the warp threads – and pull gently. Fluff out the wool between your fingers to create random uneven puffs of stitches. Continue for several rows to achieve your 'cloud' of super chunky wool. Weave in the beginning and end tails of roving between the 'clouds'.

10 Weave three rows of basic stitches with white wool below the super chunky wool to hold the 'clouds' firmly in place.

11 Cut and double up several lengths of black cotton twine, the same fibre used earlier to make the warp threads. I have cut sixty pieces of twine about twice the length of the loom, to account for folding. You are going to use these to make the fringe at the bottom of the weave. By using the same twine used for the warp, these fringes will give the impression of very long warp threads.

Tip

An easy way to create fringing of an identical length is to follow the cardboard technique (see page 86).

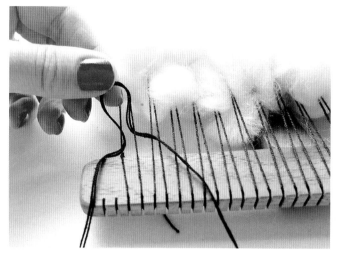

12 The technique for making the 'knotted' rya-knot fringing differs slightly from the one used for the simple rya knot (see page 42).

Combine two lengths of cut twine and then fold them in half. Pass the ends of the doubled strand under two warp threads and, with your fingers, pull the folded centre up between the two warp threads. This creates a loop of yarn above and between the warp threads.

13 Take the ends of the doubled strand and bring them through the loop, from top to bottom. Pull gently on the two ends to tighten the loop. Your 'knotted' rya knot is complete.

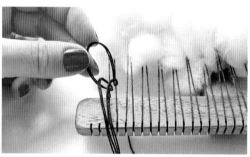

14 Continue in the same way across the full width of the weave. You might want to fold over and lay the fringes up towards the top of the frame to keep them out of your way.

Advantage of 'knotted' rya knots

This top-down rya knot is perfect if you want very fine fringing without the body: you do not need to weave any additional rows below to secure them in place (which would be visible behind the fringing) as these 'knotted' rya knots stay firmly where they are.

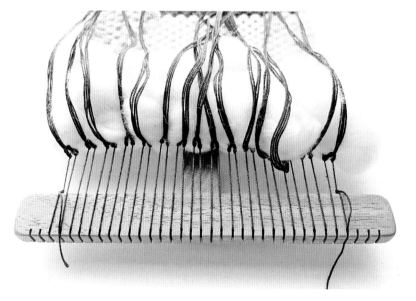

15 Cut the warp threads at the bottom of the frame and tie them together in pairs using a double knot. Knot them flat against the back of the weave to secure them.

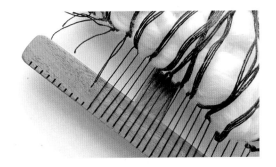

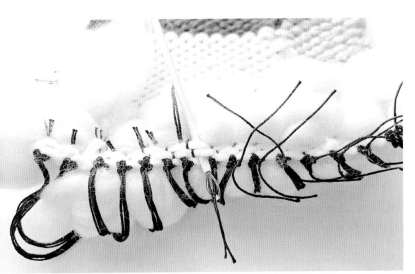

16 Work the ends of the threads into the back of the weave by threading them on to a darning needle and taking them vertically through the rows above. Cut off the excess flush against the back.

Now, you simply need to remove the weave from the loom and pass a wooden support rod through the loops. Weave it through the top loops in a pattern opposite to the stitches in the top row.

"If you do not put a support rod through the top of the weave, it will start to unravel."

55

HEM STITCH

A useful technique for securing the top or bottom of a weave is hem stitch. This leaves the warp threads visible at the top because you do not have to push the rows tightly together, or finish the weave with a support rod. It is easiest if you leave the weave on the loom; I have deliberately taken it off here to show you how the rows can unravel at the top of a weave if they have not been hemmed.

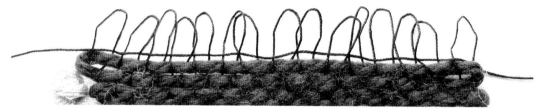

1 Take a length of twine approximately six times the width of the weave. Thread it on to your darning needle and, from the left-hand side, weave the twine all the way across the first row using the basic stitch, working opposite to the weave pattern in the row below.

2 When you have reached the final loop on the right-hand side of the weave, take the needle back behind it and wind the twine around the base of the loop, close to the weave, a few times in an anticlockwise direction. Pass the needle through the loop and pull tight. Bring it from the back of the weave to the front in between the first and second rows of the weave. Repeat the process on the next loop, as shown.

3 Continue in the same way across the full width of the weave and then finish by tying off with a knot. Weave this knot into the back of the weave and then cut off the remaining twine so that it sits flush.

Your weave is now hemmed so that the first rows do not unravel.
This is a good method if you do not want to use a support rod and if
you would like to see the top of the warp threads.

WEAVING SHAPES

Incorporating shapes makes effective, graphic weaves; simply playing with colours and materials. This weaving project will teach you two techniques: how to use a template, and how to create a shape with the warp threads for a more organic look.

TOOLS	FIBRES	STITCHES USED
1 weaving loom	1 ball of fine ecru string	basic stitch
1 darning needle	1 reel of white cotton twine	decrease and increase
1 pair of scissors	1 ball of ecru wool	shapes
1 pale-coloured marker pen	1 ball of gold metallic wool	rya loop knot
1 support rod	1 ball of purple wool	'knotted' rya knot
1 comb		
1 sheet of paper or card		

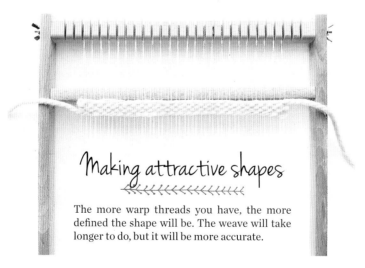

Making attractive shapes

The more warp threads you have, the more defined the shape will be. The weave will take longer to do, but it will be more accurate.

1 String the loom with a double warp using fine ecru string. Weave a few rows of ecru wool using the basic stitch.

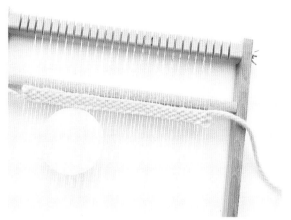

2 Cut out a circle from the paper or card and position it where you want your shape to be. Weave it over and under the warp threads to hold it in place. This template will serve as a shape for you to weave around.

3 With the marker pen, draw an irregular, snake-like shape directly on to the warp threads. Don't worry if these markings aren't neat, as they will be covered up by the yarn later on.

4 Weave the inside of the snake shape with the gold wool and a darning needle, using increases and decreases to follow your drawn outline as much as possible. Push the rows together when you have completed the shape.

5 Start by filling in the left-hand side around the circle template with ecru wool. Use increases and decreases to weave as closely as possible to the template.

Tip

If you have a more elaborate design in mind, position the paper under the loom, then transfer the pattern by tracing directly on to the warp threads.

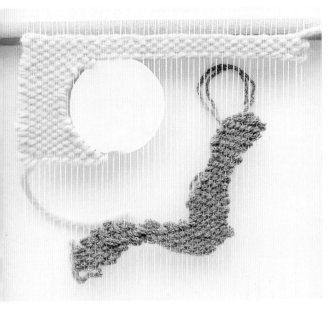

6 Weave down towards the bottom of the circle, then weave in the right-hand side of the circle, between the snake shape and the template. Fill in the area to the right of the snake shape.

You may find the rows shift a little as you weave. Don't panic: simply reposition them with your fingers.

7 Finish by weaving a few rows under both shapes, then press the rows snugly together using your fingers or a comb.

Remove the paper circle carefully so you do not spoil the rows. If necessary, carefully reposition moved rows with your fingers.

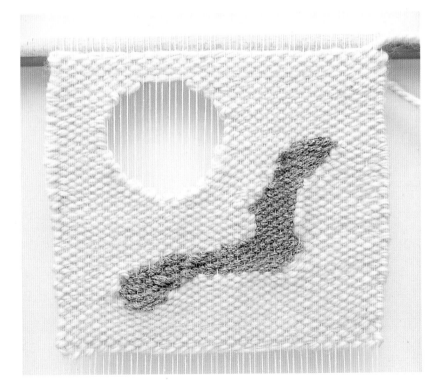

8 Fill in the empty circle with the purple wool. Use the darning needle to carefully weave the wool over and under the warp threads, making the necessary increases and decreases until it meets the ecru wool.

The spirit of nature

To give the weave a more organic effect, you could play with the tension around the edges. You don't always need to have a perfectly straight weave!

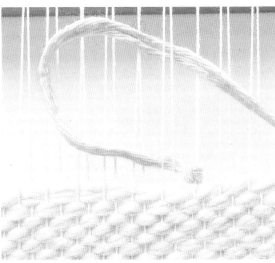

9 Rotate the weave by 180 degrees so that it is upside down. Take a long length of white cotton twine and knot one end to a warp thread, approximately halfway across the weave.

10 Make a loop that passes under two warp threads adjacent to the knot, as shown in the photo.

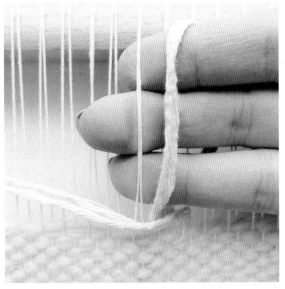

11 Bring the end of the twine over the warp threads and down to the left to make a loop.

12 Put your fingers through the loop, simultaneously picking up the next two warp threads with your hand.

13 Take the end of the twine and wrap it around the tips of your fingers, from back to front. This will give you a new loop.

14 Pull the second loop under the two warp threads lifted with your fingers. The end of the twine should stay on your left.

15 Gently pull the two loops downwards to secure them in place. You have made your first rya loop knot.

16 Continue in the same direction, repeating these steps until the end of the weave. To hold the loops in place, work a basic stitch above the fringing with another length of twine across the full width of the weave and then push it gently against the loops with a comb.

17 Turn the weave the right way up again. Weave a few more rows of twine across the whole width of the weave and fold the loops back down. Cutting through the loops will leave you with looped rya knots.

Tip

You can use the rya loop knot technique when you have a lot of fringing to do on a weave: as you work two rya knots at once, it makes fringing quicker. Once you have made the desired number of rya loops, simply snip through the ends of the loops with a pair of scissors.

18 Create a small row of long 'knotted' rya knot fringes (see page 54), using doubled twine split slightly between your fingers. Start from the far-left side of the weave, working all the way up to the row of rya loops.

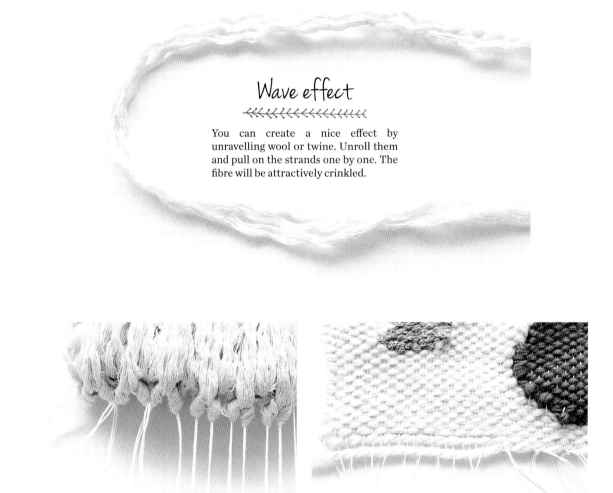

Wave effect

You can create a nice effect by unravelling wool or twine. Unroll them and pull on the strands one by one. The fibre will be attractively crinkled.

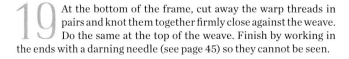

19 At the bottom of the frame, cut away the warp threads in pairs and knot them together firmly close against the weave. Do the same at the top of the weave. Finish by working in the ends with a darning needle (see page 45) so they cannot be seen.

Filling in gaps

In some areas of the weave there might be gaps, especially between the different shapes. You can leave them as they are, or fill them in using a needle and fine, corresponding yarn if they bother you. The result will be invisible if you slide the yarn discreetly between the rows.

Another method involves weaving between the rows of the two colours. Rather than turning round when you meet the join, continue to weave the new colour over the warp threads between two rows of the other colour. This will give a 'pixelated' effect along the intersection. It is up to you to choose which look you like best.

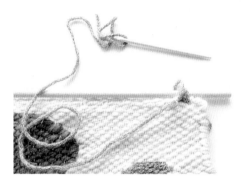

20 An alternative way of attaching your weaving to a support rod is to take a length of gold metallic wool, pass it between two warp threads, slide it under the first row of weaving and wind it several times round the wooden rod. Repeat a little way along to secure, then do the same at the other end of the rod.

Worth knowing

This method works better for smaller weaving projects. If your weave is bigger and heavier, you will need to wind the wool round the centre of the rod as well, so that the weight is better distributed.

BRAIDED (SOUMAK) WEAVES

This voluminous weave with its softly coloured plaits is a good opportunity to use natural dyes. You will learn two different ways of making a braid that you can use in weaving. Choose between the two methods depending on the thickness of the fibres you are using.

TOOLS

1 medium-sized, rectangular weaving loom
1 support rod
1 pair of scissors
1 crochet hook
1 comb

FIBRES

1 ball of white cotton twine
1 skein of ecru super chunky wool
1 skein of pink merino roving
1 skein of yellow merino roving
1 skein of beige merino roving
1 skein of ecru merino roving
1 ball of gold metallic wool

STITCHES USED

basic stitch
braid
soumak
'knotted' rya knot

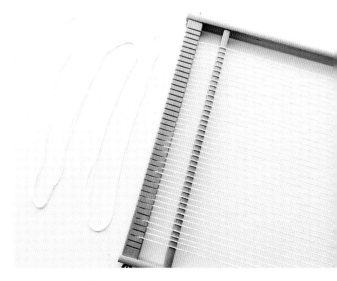

1 String the loom with single warp threads using the white cotton twine.

2 Cut a length of cotton twine eight times the width of your weave. Fold it in half.

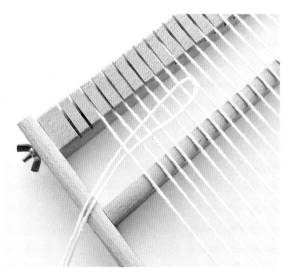

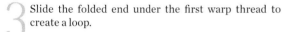

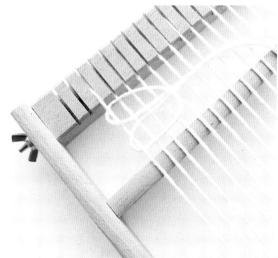

3 Slide the folded end under the first warp thread to create a loop.

4 Bring the ends of the twine through the loop, over the warp threads. Pull the knot tight.

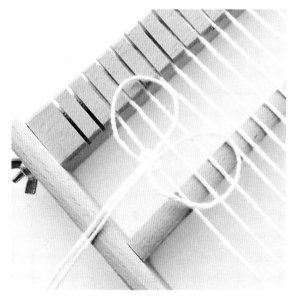

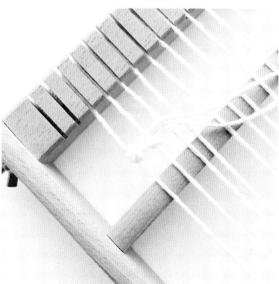

5 Pass the ends of the twine right around the second warp thread, from the front to the back. The ends will come out on the left-hand side of the loom.

6 Pull the loops tight.

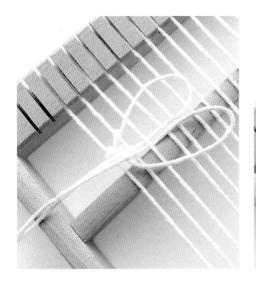

"Little by little,
the braid
will begin to
appear."

7 Take hold of the ends once again and pass them round the third warp thread. Pull tight to create another plait.

8 Repeat this step across each of the warp threads. Little by little, the braid will begin to appear.

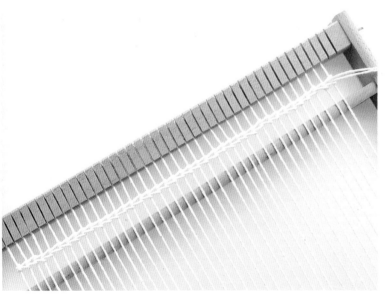

9 Continue in the same way across the full width of the weave.

10 Work in the remaining ends by weaving them between the loops of the braid, using the basic stitch. You may need to part the braid slightly to do this, as you can see above.

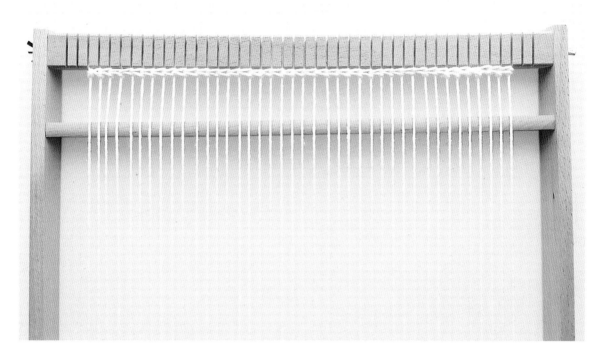

11 Push the braid snugly against the top of the loom using a comb or your fingers.

Advantages of braiding

As well as being decorative, braiding is a good way of securing the start of the weave as the fibres will not move. It is also very good to use if you wish to incorporate fairly fine fibres.

To make it quicker and easier to braid, you can thread the two ends through a needle when weaving.

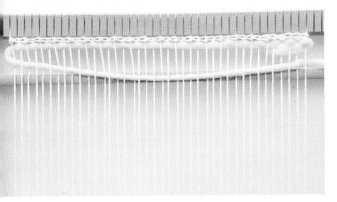

12 Start with the basic stitch in the ecru super chunky wool. Once you have woven a row, work in the tail left at the start between two rows (see also page 48), and then push the rows together.

13 Do a few more rows in the basic stitch with the ecru super chunky wool, then work in the end tail between two rows. Squeeze together snugly using a comb or your fingers.

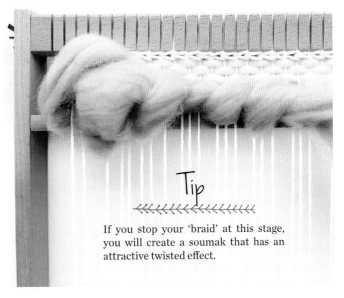

Tip

If you stop your 'braid' at this stage, you will create a soumak that has an attractive twisted effect.

14 Take the pink roving and make a loop by passing one end over three warp threads, weaving the fibre under the third warp thread and then bringing the end up between the second and third warp threads.

15 Bring the wool across the three next warp threads in the same way to create a spiral effect. Repeat until you reach the middle. You have just created a soumak weave.

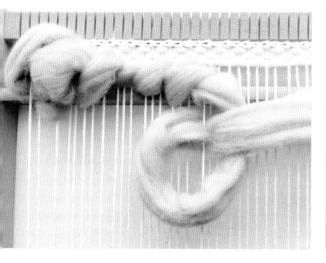

16 Change direction, wrapping the wool in the opposite way around the same warp thread as on the previous row.

17 Continue the second soumak until you are back to where you started. You have made a complete braid.

Worth knowing

Soumak braiding works well with very thick fibres.

18 Work in the ends of the wool between the rows of soumak using the basic stitch. Push the rows together.

19 Using the same ecru super chunky wool as before, weave a few rows of basic stitch next to the soumak braid to fill in the empty space.

20 Take the yellow roving and make another soumak braid, following Steps 14–18. Then, weave a few rows in the ecru super chunky wool below, using the basic stitch.

21 Weave a third, single soumak this time, using the beige roving. Note that I have placed this in the centre of the weave; this balances out the soumaks worked above.

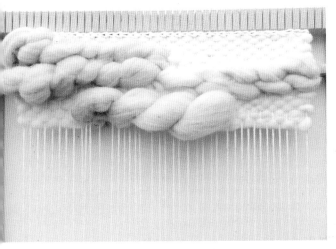

22 Fill in either side of the beige soumak with a few rows of ecru super chunky wool (see left), and then work a few more rows of ecru super chunky wool below the soumak (see right). Squeeze together regularly with fingers or a comb to keep the braids in place. On the last few rows, start to decrease the weave on the left-hand side by omitting a warp thread each time (see also pages 48 and 49).

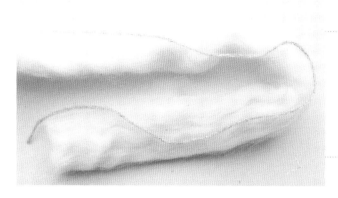

Playing with volumes

Double the roving with other fibres for a different effect. Play with textures, colours and thicknesses.

23 With a length of ecru merino roving doubled with gold metallic wool for extra interest, continue the decrease on left-hand side of the weave and work a soumak.

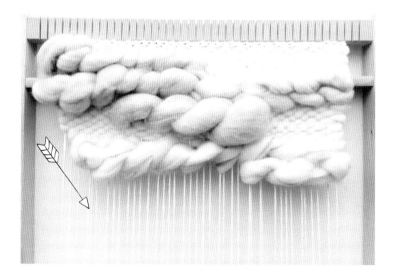

24 Weave the soumak to the far right of the weave. At the end, turn back to start a new row, but only work the soumak about a third of the way across. This will allow you to experiment with volume.

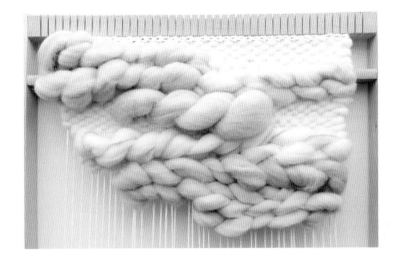

25 Continue to decrease and reduce the width of the rows on the left-hand side, alternating the fibres and their colours as you go. Weave a few rows of basic stitch between each braid with ecru super chunky wool to secure them in place. Little by little, a diagonal will appear and your weaving will take a triangular form.

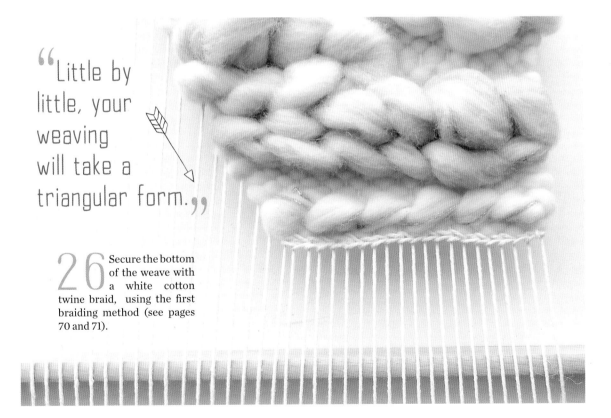

"Little by little, your weaving will take a triangular form."

26 Secure the bottom of the weave with a white cotton twine braid, using the first braiding method (see pages 70 and 71).

27 Cut long lengths of twisted ecru super chunky wool, double the length of the loom, and unravel them to achieve a crinkle effect.

28 Add fringes along the edge of the decrease using the 'knotted' rya knot technique (see page 54).

29 From time to time, knot a length of coloured roving above the crinkled wool to provide a contrast in texture.

30 Continue to add the fringing in this way, following the diagonal decrease to the bottom of the weave.

31 Cut the warp threads at the bottom two by two and knot them together in pairs flush against the weave. Remove the weave from the loom and turn it over.

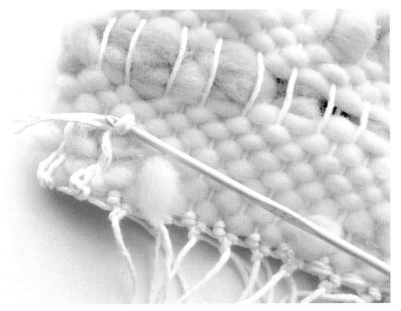

32 Work the warp threads into the weave (see pages 45). Finish by carefully weaving a support rod through the top loops, working contrary to the basic stitch pattern in the first row.

Tip

If necessary, you can use a crochet hook to work the warp threads between the rows. This is a good tool to use when the threads (or yarn) are quite thick.

FRINGED WEAVES

This sort of weaving is another way of experimenting with volume. Whether seemingly haphazard or carefully groomed, fringing can also be a good way of recycling leftover strands of wool.

TOOLS

1 large weaving loom
1 tapestry needle
1 pair of scissors
1 support rod
1 comb
1 large rectangle of cardboard (optional)

FIBRES

1 ball of thick white cotton twine
1 ball of two-tone wool
1 ball of cream T-shirt yarn
1 ball of handmade denim yarn (see page 18)
lengths of scrap wool in a variety of textures and colours

STITCHES USED

basic stitch
rya knot
twist

1 Cut a length of two-tone wool eight times the width of your weave. Bring it around the first warp thread so that it sits right in the middle of your length of wool.

2 Bring the two ends of the wool strand to the right side of the weave, crossing the lower end over the upper end as you do this.

3 With the upper strand, pass it under the second warp thread and bring it back up over the top of the rest of the weave.

4 Take the lower end and cross it over the upper strand. It has now become the upper strand.

5 Take the upper strand and pass it under the third warp thread, bringing it back up over the top of the rest of the weave. A twist will have started to form. Pull both strands tight.

6 Continue in the same way across the full width of the weave. Make sure, each time you pull the twisted strands, the space between each warp thread is the same and the tension consistent. If necessary, push the warp threads apart with your fingers to ensure that the spacing remains even.

7 When you near the end of the row, pass the upper strand of wool over the top of the lower strand, slide it under the last warp thread and bring it up over the rest of the weave to begin the next row.

8 With the lower strand, pass it over the warp thread just under the first row and then bring the end up so that it lies across the rest of weave and creates a loop. Wrap the upper strand around this lower strand and take it under the second warp thread from the right. Pass the lower strand over the second warp thread, and then cross the upper strand over it to begin the second row of twists.

9 Continue to create twists until the end of the row, then work in the ends of the yarn between the two rows.

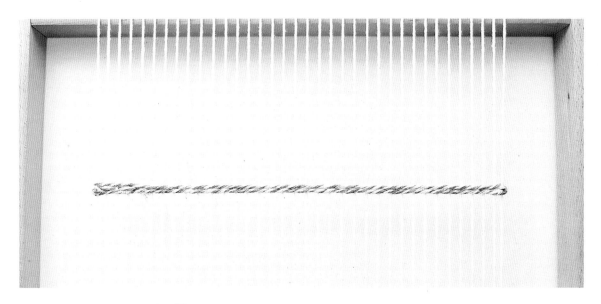

10 Squeeze the twisted rows together well, using a comb or your fingers.

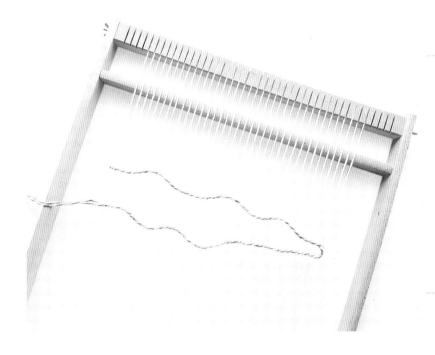

Creating shapes

Like the braid in the previous project (see pages 70 and 71), this system of twisting is useful for holding the top or bottom of the weave in place. However, you can also use it to outline and make shapes, which can then be filled in with another colour or even left empty as a 'negative space'.

11 Take some T-shirt yarn and weave several rows of basic stitch, beginning from the left-hand side. I have woven five rows. Work the beginning and end tails of yarn between two rows, and then push the cream T-shirt yarn rows together firmly to secure and create extra volume.

12 Work basic stitch in cream T-shirt yarn only three-quarters of the way along the weave, then leave a long tail hanging. Take a strip of handmade denim yarn and weave a few rows that decrease towards the left-hand side. This time, work this decrease by omitting two warp threads at every row. I have used a darning needle for ease.

13 Pick up the cream T-shirt yarn from before and weave it below the decreases.

14 Use rya knots to make some fringes below your cream rows (see also page 42). Place a length of scrap wool over two warp threads, wrap the ends around them and bring them up through the middle from back to front. Pull tight to finish the rya knot. Repeat throughout the whole weave, using a variety of yarn scraps of different types and colours. Position the fringes where you like, creating contrasts between colours, textures and materials.

Tip

Over time, put aside any leftover pieces of wool you cut off for projects in a pot or bag, so you can reuse them later for making fringes.

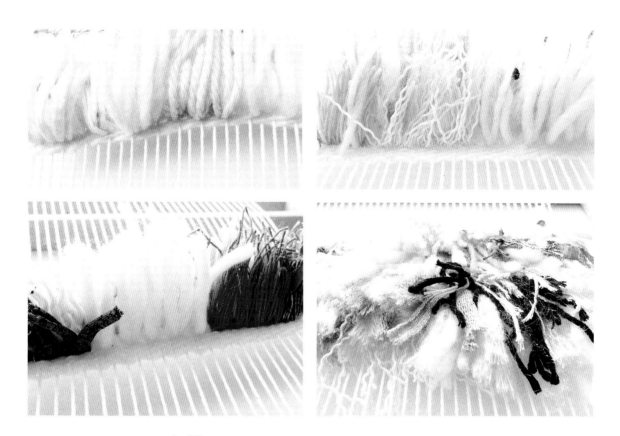

15 The secret of weaving fringes is to do a few rows of basic stitch in a length of neutral wool after each row of rya knots. I have used cream T-shirt yarn for this. Doing this keeps the fringes securely in place and will ensure that they do not come undone.

Neat fringes

A good way of making fringes of the same length quickly is to wind your chosen fibre around a piece of cardboard, cut to the desired length of the fringes, and then snip through the looped strands at the bottom – very quickly and easily, you have made your uniform fringes.

Tip

Fold the fringes back down from time to time to check how they look and make any adjustments to colours or fibres if need be.

16 Once you have finished your project, weave three rows of basic stitches in neutral wool at the bottom, directly under the last row of fringes, to hold the rest of the weave securely in place.

17 Cut the warp threads two by two and tie them in pairs flat against the weave using a double knot.

18 Remove your weaving carefully from the loom before threading it on to a support rod. The reverse side of the weave is also very attractive!

Tip

The fringe effect means you do not have to work in the warp threads; you can simply leave them hanging at the bottom of the weave. You can let the fringes fall naturally for a more organic look, or arrange them carefully to give your work a more formal appearance.

EMBROIDERED WEAVES

Embroidery is a simple technique that can give your project the look of a poetic, abstract painting. Stitch a multitude of colours, designs, geometric shapes... Anything is possible!

TOOLS

1 small weaving loom
1 darning needle
1 tapestry needle
1 support rod
1 pair of scissors
1 comb

FIBRES

1 reel of white cotton twine
1 ball of white wool
lengths of scrap wool in different colours – I have used powder-pink, light blue, mustard yellow and black metallic wool

STITCHES USED

basic stitch
'knotted' rya knot
embroidery stitches (see page 91)

1 String the loom with white cotton twine, doubled to create a tighter surface. Take a length of white wool and weave several rows in the basic stitch, starting from the right-hand side. Work in the beginning tail.

2 Once you have woven a few more rows in white wool, push the rows together so they are nice and tight; this will make it easier to embroider later.

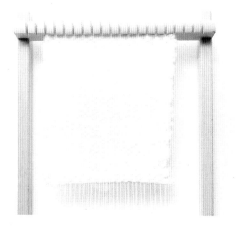

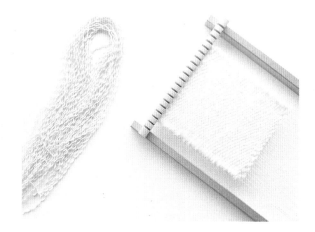

3 Continue to weave as many rows as you like, pushing them together with a comb now and then, until you have achieved the desired length.

4 Prepare the fringes using white cotton twine. Pull on the individual threads in the twine, one by one, to separate the strands and achieve a crinkled effect.

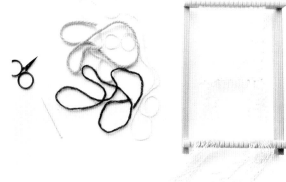

5 Add some fringes using the 'knotted' rya knot technique (see page 54) on the far-left- and far-right-hand sides of the weave. Leave the warp threads bare in the centre.

6 Now for the embroidery. Gather together the coloured threads you want to use and the tapestry needle.

Playing with colours

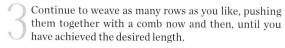

Changing the background colour of your weave is a great way to experiment with colour, and can help achieve the look you want. For example, a black background can give the weave a very graphic look.

7 Embroider the patterns and motifs of your choosing on to your weave in a variety of colours, using whatever stitches you like. I have used backstitch, running stitch, chain stitch, straight stitch and satin stitch. Avoid piercing the background yarn with the needle; try instead to insert the needle between the woven stitches.

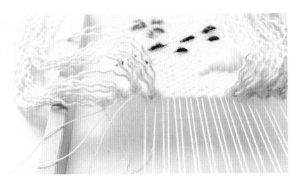

8 Cut the warp threads two by two and knot them in pairs, flush against the bottom row of your weave. Work the ends vertically into your weave with a darning needle.

9 Remove the weave from the loom and thread the wooden support rod through the loops, remembering to work alternately to the first row. If necessary, gently push the first rows up against the support rod with your fingers so they do not come loose.

WEAVING USING BARK

This project is a good opportunity to look through any natural souvenirs you have collected on a walk or a trip abroad. This particular weave is a treat for all your senses, since it smells of the materials used: hemp, pure wool and eucalyptus bark...

TOOLS

1 medium-sized weaving loom
1 piece of driftwood
1 pair of scissors
1 comb
1 darning needle

MATERIALS

1 ball of hemp yarn
1 ball of cotton yarn
1 skein of cream super chunky wool
1 skein of ecru merino roving
several strips of eucalyptus bark

STITCHES USED

basic stitch
braid
soumak

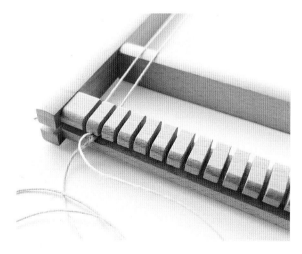

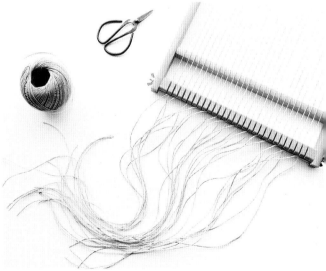

1 Begin by cutting several lengths of hemp yarn, four times the length of your loom, and fold each one in half. Starting from the top of the loom, wrap the folded end around the first two notches and then take the ends down through the bottom notches directly below. Knot the ends at the base of the loom, between these two notches, and leave the remaining ends hanging freely.

2 Repeat this stage across the full width of the loom. Not only do you now have your warp threads in place, but also some hemp fringing.

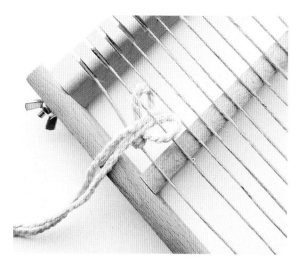

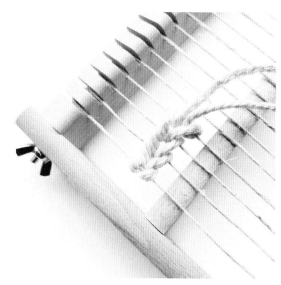

3 Start with a braid in cotton yarn (see also pages 70 and 71). With a folded length of yarn, take the folded end under the first warp thread to create a loop and then bring the ends of the yarn through the loop. Pull the knot tight. Bring the ends over the next warp thread, around and then through the middle of the strands. Pull tight. Repeat on the second warp thread.

4 Repeat this process with the third warp thread and so on. The plait will take shape little by little. Pull the yarn ends with each plait to tighten the shape.

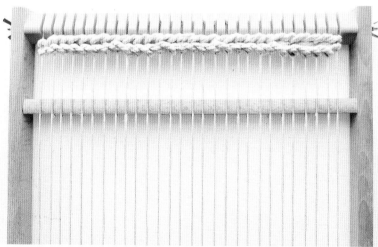

5 Continue in the same way across the full width of the weave.

6 Work the ends of the yarn in with the basic stitch, down the centre of the braid. You may need to part the braid slightly to do this. Push the braid together once this is done, up to the top of the loom.

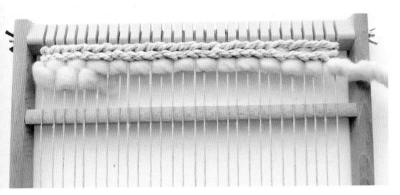

7 Using the cream super chunky wool, weave a few rows of basic stitches. Work in the beginning tail between the rows to achieve a neat finish.

8 Continue to weave more rows in basic stitch, gradually decreasing to the left-hand side. Squeeze the rows together gently, but try to allow the warp threads to show through for visual interest.

9 Fill in the empty area on the right using the ecru merino roving, taking it right up to the rows of cream super chunky wool. Weave randomly around the warp threads to create a cloud-like effect. Alternatively, work a soumak weave (see page 73).

10 When the rows of wool and roving are level, thread a strip of eucalyptus bark between the warp threads.

Worth knowing

If the piece of bark is strong enough, thread it once over, once under, the warp threads. If the wood is fragile and likely to snap, pass it over and under two or three warp threads at a time to reduce the pressure on it.

11 Using cotton yarn, weave several rows in basic stitch below the bark that steadily decrease towards the right-hand side. Push the rows together now and then with your fingers so that the eucalyptus bark is held securely in place. Try to work with the shape of the bark: as mine are bent upwards slightly, I worked an increasing row underneath initially, to support the bark; once the stitches could be worked across the full width of the weave, I then began the decrease.

Natural inspiration

For an alternative natural look, replace the bark with leaves or dried flowers. Be careful when weaving them through as they are more fragile.

12 Place another strip of bark between the warp threads, below the cotton yarn decrease. I have used a smaller piece this time.

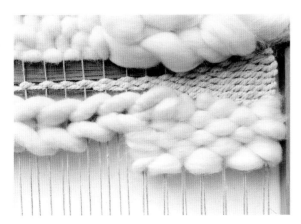

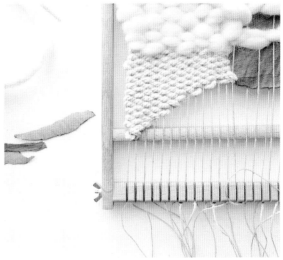

13 Weave a braid three-quarters of the way along the weave with cream super chunky wool, this time over two warp threads to accommodate the thickness of the yarn. Work a few rows of basic stitch with the chunky wool on just the right-hand side of the weave, passing over and under two warp threads at a time, then push them together with your fingers. This method means there is less tension and the warp threads will no longer show once that area has been woven.

14 Continue to fill in the rest of your weave. Use your imagination, incorporating various shapes and materials and alternating between different fibres and stitches.

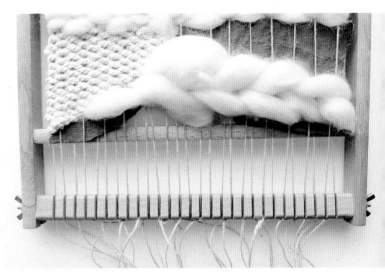

15 To give a bit of texture and balance to the composition, weave a thick soumak from ecru merino roving, winding the wool around the warp threads. As the wool is thick, feed it over three warp threads before wrapping it around.

16 Work another soumak below, in the opposite direction. The braid takes shape when you push the two rows of soumak together.

My advice

Using only natural materials makes a very free-form, impressive weave.

Don't give too much thought to how it will turn out; weave your piece almost unconsciously and automatically, and let your hands and instinct guide you around the loom.

Don't think too hard about straight edges or accurate shapes – the charm of this project lies in its more spontaneous, organic look.

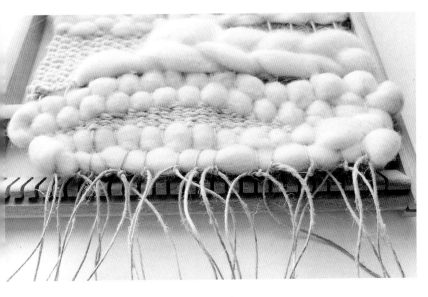

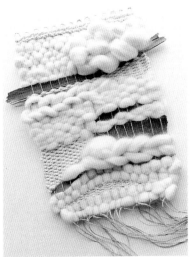

17 As you made the fringes earlier, at the beginning of the weave, now all you need to do is fill in the weave down to the knots at the bottom of the loom. You can lift the weave gently off the loom as you near the edge, to ensure that you work right up to the knots.

18 Remove your weave completely from the loom.

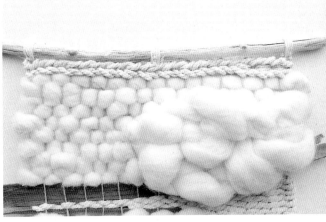

19 Using your fingers, carefully push the rows up at the bottom of the weave to hide the loops at the top – don't worry about your weave distorting, as it is held securely in place by the braid.

20 Thread a darning needle with some twine and attach your weave to the driftwood support rod (see also page 67 for guidance on how to do this). The weave will be heavy, so make sure it is attached in the centre, as well as at the ends, to prevent it from sagging.

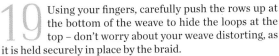

CIRCULAR WEAVING

Weaving in the round is a fun alternative to rectangular weaving. The technique is similar to rectangular weaving and the process identical, but circular looms create designs with a touch of originality.

TOOLS

1 circular loom
1 darning needle
1 pair of scissors
1 lampshade ring

FIBRES

1 ball of white cotton twine
1 ball of fluffy wool
1 ball of fluorescent pink yarn
1 ball of handmade grey T-shirt yarn (see page 18)
lengths of scrap teal yarn
lengths of scrap green yarn
1 skein of ecru merino roving

STITCHES USED

basic stitch
'knotted' rya knot
braid
soumak

1 Make a circular loom (see page 25) and string the warp threads (see page 30). Thread a darning needle with fluffy wool and bring a length of wool up through the middle, down and under the centre of crossed twine and then up on the other side.

2 Start weaving using the basic over-under stitch. It doesn't matter where you begin; the 'rows' are created in spiral fashion, and the fact that there is an odd number of warp threads means you will find yourself working automatically contrary to the previous 'row'.

3 Weave several rounds of fluffy wool, then turn the whole thing over and knot the ends to a warp thread to secure. You will not be able to see the knot at all from the front.

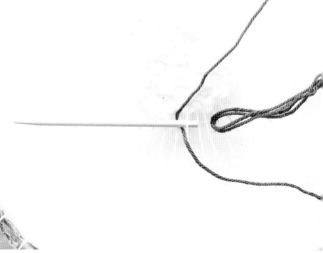

4 Flip the weave back to the right side. Take the fluorescent pink yarn, double it and pass it around the warp thread subsequent to the one you knotted before with the fluffy wool. This makes a seamless join in both colour and stitch.

5 You are going to work braiding around the circle of fluffy wool, using the pink yarn. To weave the braid quickly, thread the ends of the pink yarn through a darning needle.

6 Take the yarn over and around the next warp thread and then back through the middle of the doubled yarn (see also pages 70 and 71) Pull gently on the ends. You have now made your first loop.

7 Continue in the same way right around the weave until you have completed one round of pink. Cut the yarn, leaving a 5cm (2in) tail.

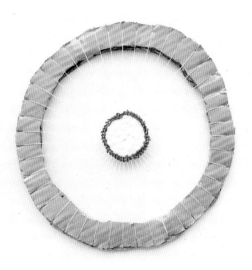

8 On the reverse side of the loom, knot the beginning and end tails around the warp thread and tuck it gently under and up through one stitch of fluffy wool. You will have a little bump at this spot but this will disappear when you weave the following rows.

9 Knot the grey T-shirt yarn around the same warp thread on the reverse side of the weave.

10 Flip over the loom and weave in the grey T-shirt yarn using the basic stitch.

11 Weave several rounds, then knot it around a warp thread on the reverse side of the loom in the same way as the other fibres (see Steps 3 and 8 on pages 102 and 103).

12 Prepare the fringes by combining multiple lengths of teal and green yarn.

13 To make a 'knotted' rya knot on a circular loom, pass the strands under two warp threads and then pinch them up through the centre with your thumb and forefinger to make a loop.

14 Pass both ends of the combined teal and green yarn through the loop from top to bottom. Secure the rya knot by pulling gently on the ends.

15 Repeat this stage several times along subsequent warp threads on one side, to achieve a nice dense effect with the fringing. Once this is done, secure the fringes with a few rounds of grey T-shirt yarn using the basic stitch.

16 With the ecru merino roving, take it over three warp threads and then bring the end back up between the second and third warp threads to finish the spiral (see also page 73). Repeat this stage all the way round to complete the soumak weave.

17 Once you have completed a round of soumak, weave a round of basic stitches using merino roving. Push the rows tightly together with your fingers. Automatically, a neat braid has been formed.

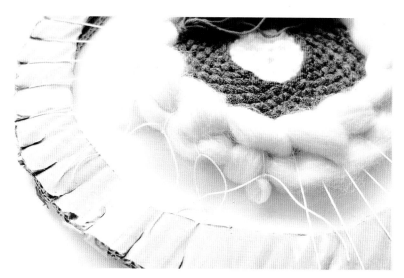

18 Cut the warp threads two by two, knotting them together in pairs and pulling tight so they are flush against the weave. As you have an odd number of warp threads, your final knot will consist of three warp threads tied together.

19 Work in the remaining warp thread tails between the rounds on to the reverse side of the weave, using a darning needle.

Tip

You can hang up your completed weave as it is, but to give it more support I recommend attaching it to a circular frame – lampshade rings fit the bill perfectly. Using a darning needle threaded with twine, pass the thread through the weave between a wrap and weft thread, then wind it around the ring. Continue all the way round and knot the thread on the reverse side.

20 Arrange the fringing with your fingers so that it falls nicely.

WEAVING WITHOUT A LOOM

It is not essential to have weaving tools and accessories at home to create an attractive wall hanging – a simple tangle of wool can sometimes create an interesting effect! Here is how to weave without a loom.

TOOLS

1 pair of scissors
1 support rod
1 crochet hook (optional)

FIBRES

1 skein of cream super chunky wool
1 skein of grey super chunky wool
1 ball of powder-pink wool (optional)

STITCHES USED

lark's head knot
basic stitch
'knotted' rya knot
tassel (optional)

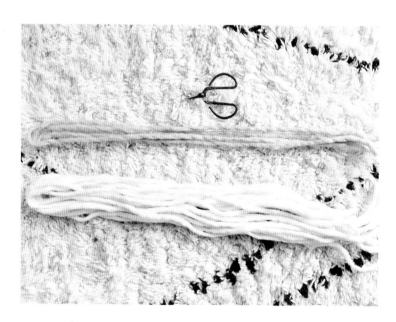

1 To create a big weave, set yourself up comfortably on a rug. Prepare the lengths of different wools. Depending on how big you would like your weave to be, these can be as long or short as you like.

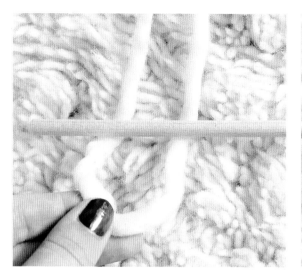

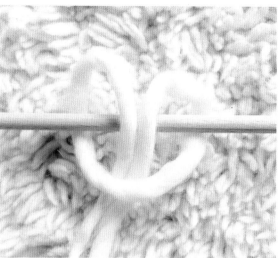

2 Fold a length of cream super chunky wool in half, and pass the folded end under the centre of the support rod.

3 Take the ends and bring them over the top of the support rod and down through the loop formed by the folded wool.

4 Tighten the knot by pulling on the ends. You have made a lark's head knot, and these yarn ends will be your first two warp threads.

5 Continue in the same way right along the support rod. Vary the colours as you go.

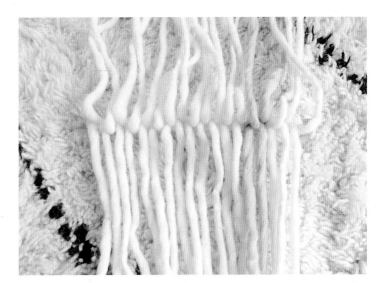

6 Along the support rod, flip and fold upwards alternate strands of super chunky wool.

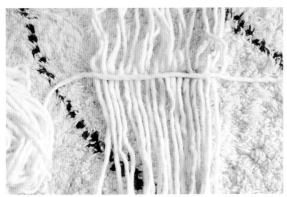

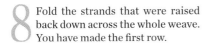

7 Take your skein of cream super chunky wool. Leaving a 5cm (2in) tail on the right, lay a length of wool across the warp threads, just below this point.

8 Fold the strands that were raised back down across the whole weave. You have made the first row.

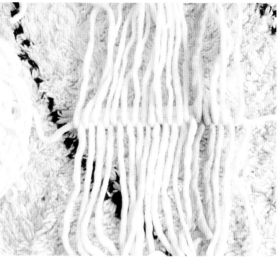

9 Fold alternate strands of super chunky wool upwards again, but this time the other way around: if you raised the odd warp threads on the previous row, raise the even warp threads this time.

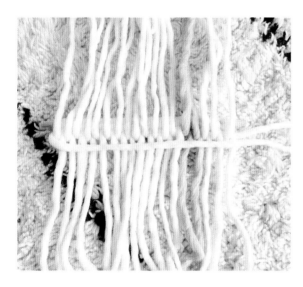

10 Unroll another length of cream wool from the skein and lay it across the width of the weave to make a second row.

11 Fold the strands that were raised back down and flip up the alternate strands. Repeat Steps 6 to 10 all the way down the weave. Push the rows together with your fingers as you go, so the weave is sufficiently tight.

 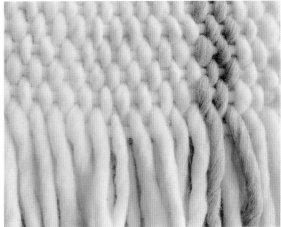

12 There may still be holes in the weave, or perhaps you would like the edges to be straighter. If so, use your fingers to pull gently on the loops of weft yarn along the sides, to make the weave tighter where you think it is too loose. To ensure that the weave is consistently taut throughout, continue to pull on each row until you reach the bottom of the weave.

13 Once this is done, squeeze the rows together by hand, pushing them upwards one by one and little by little.

14 The weave is now tight and the edges should be straight.

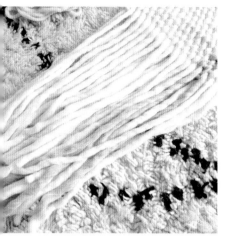  

15 You could leave the weave as it is at this point, knotting the warp threads in pairs. Alternatively, you can add fringes to give it more volume.

16 Prepare the fringes by taking two long strands of cream wool and doubling them. Fold them in half, then pull the folded centre up between the first two warp threads. Take the ends through the loop and then pull tight to form a 'knotted' rya knot (see also page 54).

17 Tie a double knot with the warp threads underneath to hold the bottom of the weave and the fringing securely in place. Continue in the same way across the full width of the weave.

18 When the fringing and knotting are completed, turn the whole thing over to start working in the tails.

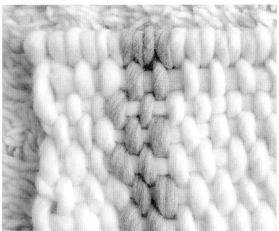

19 Work the tails in with your fingers, weaving them carefully through the warp threads. If you find this tricky to do with your fingers, you could use a crochet hook: push the hook end through the intended stitch, grab the tail and pull it through. Repeat along successive stitches until the tail is completely woven in.

Despite the thickness of the wool, you won't be able to see the ends that you have worked in either on the front or back of the weave.

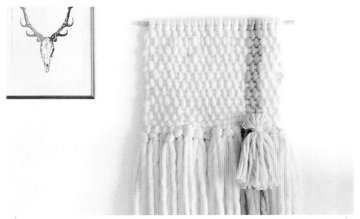

Using tassels

If you have used mostly neutral shades, you can give your weave a bit of extra colour and flair by decorating it with tassels. Make a tassel with the pink wool (see pages 22 and 23) and pass another pink strand through the loop at the top. Pass either end of the strand round the warp threads and knot it tightly at the back of the weave to secure the tassel in place.

MACRAMÉ CLOUD WEAVE

So soft, this adorable little woven cloud is perfect for the wall of a child's bedroom. This project uses two complementary techniques: macramé and weaving. Sweet dreams!

TOOLS

1 support rod
1 pair of scissors
1 roll of masking tape

FIBRES

1 ball of natural string
1 skein of ecru merino roving

STITCHES USED

basic stitch
lark's head knot
soumak
macramé

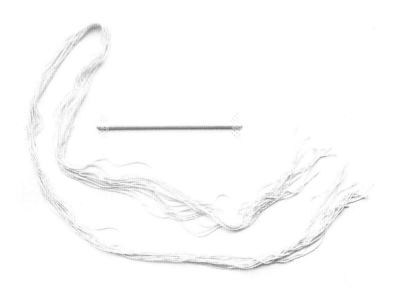

1 Attach the wooden support rod to a table using masking tape. Allow a little space so you can pass the string around it.

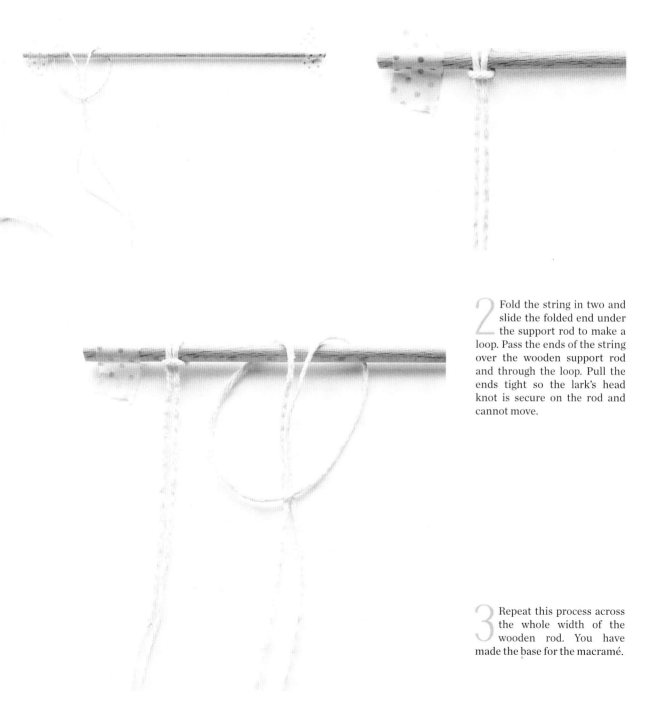

2 Fold the string in two and slide the folded end under the support rod to make a loop. Pass the ends of the string over the wooden support rod and through the loop. Pull the ends tight so the lark's head knot is secure on the rod and cannot move.

3 Repeat this process across the whole width of the wooden rod. You have made the base for the macramé.

Worth knowing

To ensure that your macramé is a success, tie an even number of threads to the support rod. I worked sixteen lark's head knots along the rod, making thirty-two warp threads in total.

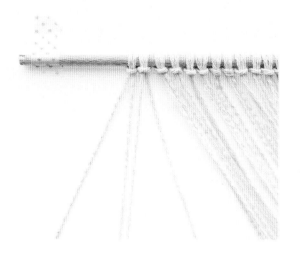

4 To make the first knot, pull out the first string on the left and the fourth on the right. This leaves you with two in the centre.

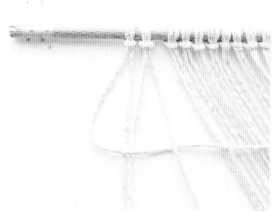

5 Pass the first string over the two threads in the centre and then under the fourth. This makes a '4' shape.

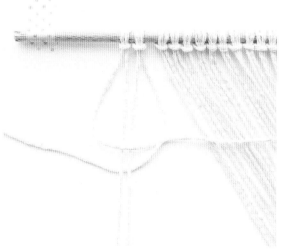

6 Now pass the fourth string over the first string and then under the two in the middle, towards the left.

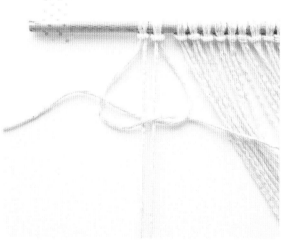

7 Take the end of the fourth string and pass it through the loop to the left of the centre threads, from back to front. It should finish up over the top of the first string. You have just created a half knot.

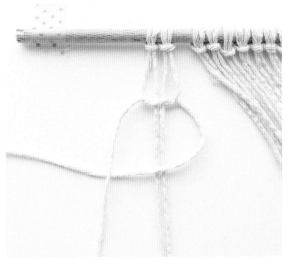

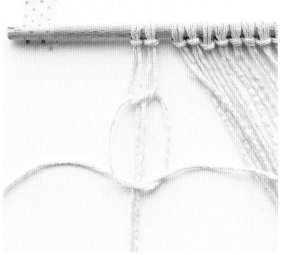

8 Tighten the knot and repeat the process but in reverse. Your first string is now in the fourth position. Bring it over the two strings in the middle, then under the fourth string which is now in the first position.

9 Pass the fourth strand, which is now in the first position, under the two middle strands and through the loop, from back to front.

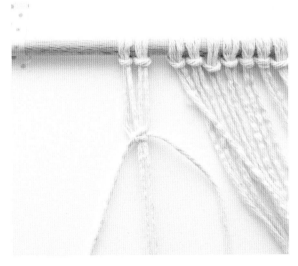

10 Pull the second knot tight over the first. You have just completed your first square knot.

11 Repeat these steps with the remaining threads, so you end up with square knots across the full width of the weave.

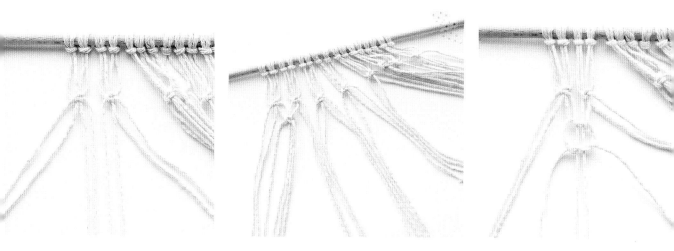

12   For the next row of flat knots, separate four strands once again, but this time ignore the two strands at either end (see top left image). Perform each stage of the flat knot with these strands, pull tight and repeat with the next four strands.

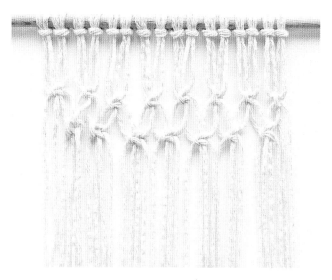

13   Form flat knots across the whole width of the weave. They will be offset from those on the previous row.

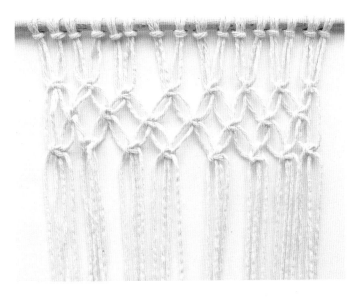

14 Weave the third row of square knots in line with the knots on the first row, simply by going back to knotting the first four strands together as in Step 12.

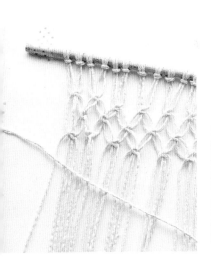

15 Cut a new length of string and position it across the macramé. Attach one end to the table with masking tape to secure.

16 Wind the first strand on the far-left side of the weave (weaving strand) around the new length of string (attached strand) from back to front. The weaving strand should come out on the left.

17 Take the end of the weaving strand and pass it over the attached string.

18 With the weaving strand, make another loop around the attached string, over and around, bringing the end out to the left.

19 Tighten the two loops around the attached string.

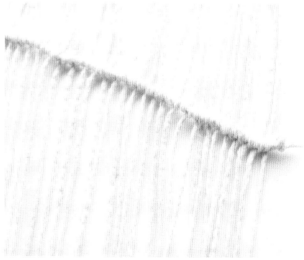

20 Perform these steps with each of the hanging strings across the whole width of the macramé. Note the deliberate angle of the knots.

21 To finish, tie a double knot at each end and then snip off the excess so the ends are flush with the weave.

22 Make a second row of knots with another length of string. Note the angle of this second line veers down to the left side. These two lines will mark the beginning and end of your soumak weave later.

23 Below your last row of knots, create a spiral of threads with your first four warp threads. To do this, tie a continuous line of knots, approximately 10–12.75cm (4–5in) long. These are made simply by working multiple half knots (see page 120).

24 Create spirals across the full width of the macramé.

25 Now link the first two spirals. Separate the strands and bring together the four middle ones, setting aside the first two to the left and the last two to the right.

26 Tie a square knot following the instructions in Steps 4–10 (see pages 120 and 121).

27 Link the strands in the second spiral to those in the third by bringing together the two strands you had set aside to the right earlier and knotting them with the first two strands of the third spiral (see also Step 12 on page 122 for further guidance). Continue in the same way across the full width of the weave.

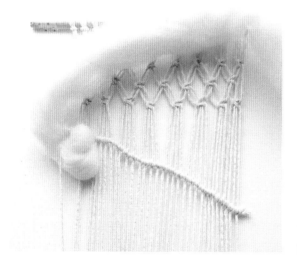

28 The space where you are going to weave your soumak is between the two lines of macramé knots. Take a length of ecru merino roving and take it under the first warp thread to secure the end.

29 Weave the roving around the fourth warp thread and up between the third and fourth warp threads. Start to weave a soumak braid (see also page 73), spacing out twists of wool randomly.

30 Continue to weave the soumak between the macramé row in a circular pattern, weaving from the outside inwards. As you go over and under around the centre, the wool will be bulkier and create a cloud-like effect. Work extra twists of soumak randomly to emphasize this, if necessary.

HANGING VASE

This project perfectly combines two passions of mine: weaving and house plants. The vase is easy to make and you can use all sorts of materials, colours and weaving techniques to make it more unique.

TOOLS

1 recycled glass jar
1 roll of masking tape
1 darning needle
1 pair of scissors

FIBRES

1 ball of white cotton string
1 reel of natural cotton twine
1 ball of handmade denim yarn (see page 18)
1 skein of banana fibre

STITCHES USED

basic stitch
rya knot
circular weaving

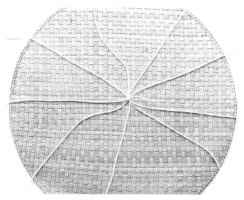

1 To make the warp threads, cut some strands of similar length from the white cotton string – use the glass jar to calculate the lengths you require. Arrange them into 'pizza slices'. In the photo, there are five pieces of string in total which, laid across one another, gives us ten strands.

2 Take one of the lengths of string and knot it at the point where the strands intersect; now the centre cannot move. Snip off one end of the length. This gives an uneven number of strands, and will make weaving in the round easier: where you have gone over a warp thread in one round, you will automatically go underneath it in the next.

3 Place the glass jar in the centre of your warp threads, bring them up and then pop the ends inside. To hold the warp threads in place while weaving, secure all the threads with masking tape, stuck along the top of the jar. Make sure the spaces in between the threads are roughly equidistant.

4 Knot the natural cotton twine in the centre to secure. Using a darning needle, start to weave the basic stitch. Do not worry about any hanging tails of twine; they will be hidden under the weft later and will not be seen.

5 When you have finished, simply knot the end to one of the warp threads. Push the rounds together with your fingers to create a more even finish. The knot will be invisible once the weave is finished.

6 You will make a line of fringes on either side of your woven vase, to add texture and interest. To make a fringe, work rya knots on the warp threads as you would for a rectangular weave (see also page 42).

7 With the knot in place, take a new length of natural twine and to its right weave basic stitch halfway round the vase. With a new length of twine, create another rya knot fringe on the opposite side of the vase. Work another strip of basic stitch in a new length of twine to complete the circle. Weave a round of basic stitch above to secure the fringes.

Repeat this process all the way to the top of the vase, creating a column of rya knots on either side, one above the other, and weaving several strips and rounds of basic stitch in between to fill the gaps and secure the fringes. You can change the colours and fibres as often as you like. In the photograph to the left I have used banana fibre, which I later follow with handmade denim yarn.

8 Once you have finished weaving, take off the masking tape and knot the warp threads in pairs. As you have an uneven number of warp threads, your remaining knot will consist of three strands. Using a darning needle, weave in any hanging tails of yarn behind the weft for a better finish.

To hang the vase, take some string and knot it around two warp threads hidden inside the weave.

WOVEN NECKLACE

Your weaving projects are not restricted to your walls. A woven necklace can be a delightful piece of jewellery to accessorize an outfit. Simply vary the colours or add a few beads to create myriad accessories that you will want to wear every day. These mini weaves could also be used as Christmas-tree decorations, or to make a mobile for a child's bedroom!

TOOLS

1 mini loom
1 darning needle
1 pair of scissors
1 roll of duct tape
1 piece of cardboard
paper scissors

FIBRES

1 reel of natural cotton twine
1 ball of gold metallic wool
1 ball of ecru super chunky wool
1 ball of natural cotton string
1 ball of white cotton string

STITCHES USED

basic stitch
'knotted' rya knot

1 Make a mini loom from a piece of cardboard. Strengthen the edges with masking tape and then cut notches along both short ends, 1cm (½in) apart.

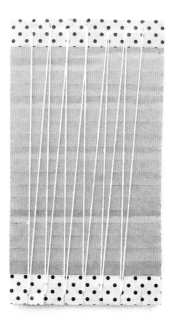

2 Starting from the top left, warp your loom using doubled thread. Divide the threads over the first two notches and then take both ends through a single notch at the bottom. Repeat along the full width of the loom. Note that the last notch is empty – this is correct.

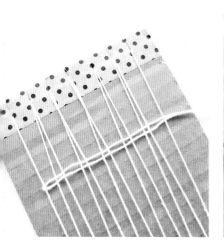

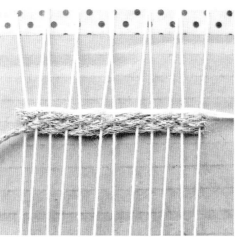

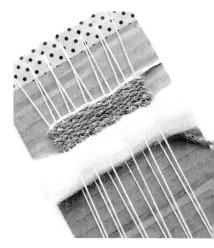

3 Weave two rows of basic stitch with doubled cotton twine. Use your fingers to ensure that they are evenly spaced. This strand will be removed at the end of the weave.

4 Below these rows, weave ten to twelve rows of basic stitch using the gold metallic wool.

5 Weave a length of ecru super chunky wool below the gold wool, working alternately to the stitches in the previous row. Snip each end. Weave a few more rows in gold wool below this ecru band.

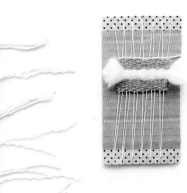
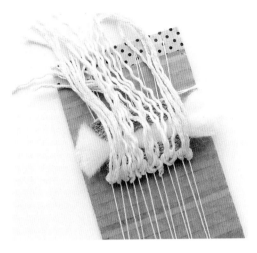

6 Prepare the fringing by cutting several lengths of different types of fibre. I have used a combination of natural and white cotton string.

7 Attach the lengths using 'knotted' rya knots (see page 54) across the full width of the weave.

8 Cut the warp threads two by two and tie each pair tightly in a double knot flush against the weave to hold the bottom of the weave in place. Work the ends into the back with a darning needle.

9 Remove the weave gently from the loom, along with the anchor strand of twine in Step 3. Knot the warp threads in pairs at the top of the weave. Work the ends into the back.

10 Take a length of string, cut it to the desired length and knot it to the first and last warp threads along the top at the back of the weave.

WOVEN DREAM-CATCHER

A circular weave, some fringing soft colours... In Native American culture, the dream-catcher prevents bad dreams from disturbing your sleep.

TOOLS

1 circular weaving loom
1 lampshade ring
1 pair of scissors
1 darning needle

FIBRES

1 ball of gold metallic wool
1 skein of ecru super chunky wool
1 skein of ecru merino roving
1 skein of pink super chunky wool
1 ball of black speckled wool
1 ball of cotton yarn

STITCHES USED

basic stitch
decreasing and increasing
'cloud' texture effect
braid
soumak
'knotted' rya knot

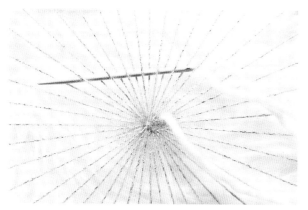

1 String the loom using the gold metallic wool. Knot the ecru super chunky wool in the centre underneath.

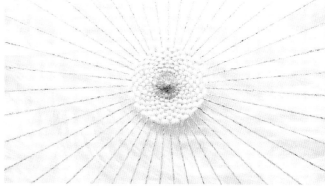

2 Weave a few rounds of basic stitch using ecru super chunky wool. Push the rows snugly together with your fingers.

Tip

Warping with coloured threads is a simple, subtle way of providing a weave with a touch of originality.

3 Take a length of ecru merino roving. Make a loop over three warp threads, and then bring the end up between the second and third warp threads.

4 Pull the loop tight.

5 Repeat this step over the next three warp threads to start forming a soumak.

6 Pull the loop tight to create the second twist in the soumak.

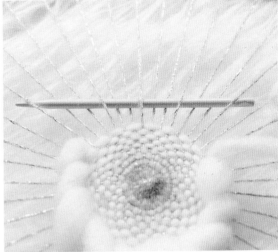

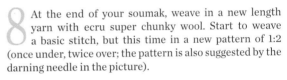

7 Continue to work the soumak weave about two-thirds of the way around the circle of basic stitches.

8 At the end of your soumak, weave in a new length yarn with ecru super chunky wool. Start to weave a basic stitch, but this time in a new pattern of 1:2 (once under, twice over; the pattern is also suggested by the darning needle in the picture).

9 Weave until you meet the end of the soumak, then turn back on yourself and continue the 1:2 pattern (once under, twice over) in the opposite direction. This builds up the ecru super chunky wool to the height of the soumak.

10 On the next row start the 1:2 pattern again, now staggering it to the right by one warp thread. Weave a few rows in this way, working up to and no further than the merino roving, and with each new round starting on the next warp thread to the right. Little by little a pattern will form, reminiscent of a spiral galaxy.

11 At the one end of your finished, staggered stitches, pass an end of pink super chunky wool between the rows of ecru super chunky wool and merino roving, and then knot to a woven warp thread at the back of the weave.

12 Weave a few of the warp threads with the pink wool, using basic stitch. Do not go all the way round: where you meet the other side of the ecru super chunky wool, turn back on yourself and weave to the start of the ecru wool band.

13 Wedge the end of the pink wool between the two rounds you've just woven and knot it to a warp thread at the back.

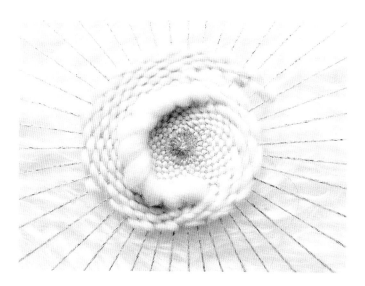

14 Repeat Steps 11–13 for several rounds, incorporating decreases and increases to make a unique, round pattern with your pink wool.

Freehand

Let your hands lead the way and see what shapes they come up with. The more random they are, the more attractive the swirl effect will look. Here, I have filled in some of the decreased and increased sections of the weave with black speckled wool.

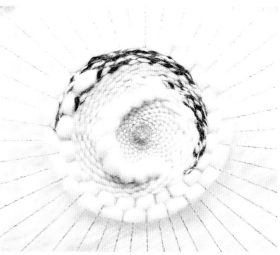

15 Using basic stitch, weave some rounds of ecru merino roving to fill in the gaps formed by the increases.

16 Push the rounds together now and then with your fingers to keep the weaving consistent.

17 Work a few basic stitches in the roving. Create a 'cloud' effect with them by pinching the stitches up gently with your thumb and forefinger.

18 Continue to fill in the rest of your weave in this way, alternating the different colours and yarns in basic stitch and throwing in decreases and increases where you see fit. When you have finished, wind a full round of soumak around the edge and then work a final round of basic stitch on the very outer edge to secure.

19 Cut the warp threads and knot them tightly in pairs, flush against the weave. The last knot will contain three warp threads. Work the remaining tails up into the rounds on the reverse side of the weave with a tapestry needle.

20 Decorate a lampshade ring by winding gold metallic wool around it.

21 Attach the weave to the lampshade ring with the gold metallic wool, using a needle. However, you will need to work between the warp threads so you do not spoil the rows. Start by knotting the gold wool to an outer warp thread on the weave. Take the threaded needle over and under the lampshade ring, and bring it back up to the weaving and make another knot on the next warp thread. Repeat all the way around the ring. Note that a triangular pattern will automatically form as you sew.

22 Prepare the fringing using a combination of all your different fibres.

23 Following the 'knotted' rya knot technique (see page 54), knot bunches of strands along one-third of your circle.

24 Create random combinations with your different bunches of fibres, to tailor your fringes to the look you want: mix thinner fibres with thicker ones, and pair two different colours together per bunch. If you wish, make the fringes different lengths too as I have done (see page 137), to add further texture and interest to your weave.

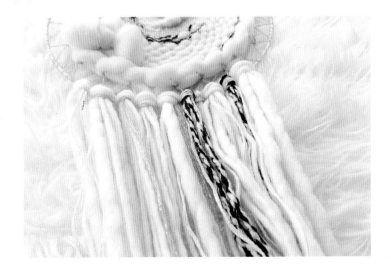

WOVEN CLUTCH BAG

The fabulous thing about weaving is that it can be used to make objects that you will use in everyday life. This project is a soft, fluffy clutch for carrying your essentials on a night out.

TOOLS

1 large rectangular weaving loom
1 darning needle
1 pair of scissors
1 comb
1 sewing needle
1 set of pins

FIBRES

1 reel of white cotton twine
1 ball of handmade denim yarn (see page 18)
1 ball of fur-effect wool
1 reel of sewing thread

STITCHES USED

basic stitch
hem stitch

EXTRA SEWING ITEMS

1 zip fastener
1 square of fabric
1 imitation silver leather ribbon
1 sewing machine with zipper foot (optional)

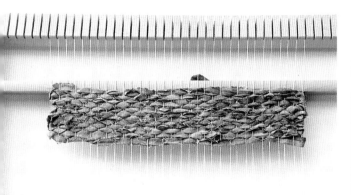

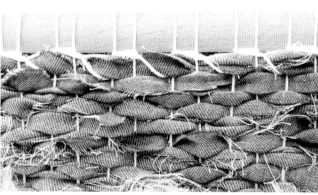

1 Weave several rows of basic stitches using the denim yarn. This band can be as thick as you wish, depending on how big you would like your clutch to be. Press the rows together using a comb so there are no visible gaps.

2 To hold the top of the weave securely in place, as this edge will become the top of your bag, work a row of hem stitch (see page 56) using a length of white cotton twine, the same used for the warp.

3 When you have completed the desired number of denim rows, swap to the fur-effect wool. Weave several rows with your wool. As the fur-effect wool is very fine, you will need to do lots of rows, pushing them together frequently so there are no gaps.

The fur effect can make it a little difficult to see what you are doing. You can always turn the weave over for a better overview.

Tip

If you are using a big loom, consider threading the wool on to a shuttle; this will make it easier to go left and right across the width of the loom.

4 To finish, weave an equal number of denim rows as you did at the beginning. The weave must be symmetrical since it will be folded in half, in the middle of the fur-effect wool, to form the bag. As you did for the top of the weave, work a row of hem stitch using a length of white cotton twine.

Worth knowing

The band of fur-effect wool must be wider than the denim bands. To help you to balance the bands and visualize the final look of the bag, hide half the weave with a sheet of paper.

5 Cut the warp threads and tightly knot them in pairs, flush against the weave. Use the needle to work in the remaining warp tails, weaving them vertically through the rows of the weave on the reverse side.

6 For a simple clutch, fold the weave in half, right sides together. Make sure they are well aligned along the edges. Pin the sides of your bag.

Sew up the sides by hand with a needle and thread, or use a sewing machine – whichever you prefer!

Once you have sewn up the sides, turn the bag the right way out. Your clutch is now ready.

MAKING FABRIC LINING

For a more finished result, add a fabric lining to your bag to give it more shape along with a zip fastener, to keep your bits and pieces safe.

1 Cut a piece of fabric to the same size as your weave.

2 Place the weave in front of you, right side facing up. Place the zip fastener along the top edge, zipper facing down, and then place the lining on top, wrong side facing up. Pin into place along one edge of the zip.

3 Stitch the layers together along this first zip edge, by hand or using the sewing machine fitted with the special zip presser foot.

4 Bring the bottom edge of the weave up to the other side of the zip fastener, right sides together, and then do the same with the lining. Pin and sew along the second side of the zip.

5 Lay your lining on one side and the weave on the other. Pin the sides of the weave right sides together and stitch.

6 Pin together the edges of the lining, right sides together and sew along one short and one long side only. Keep the remaining short side open so you can turn the bag the right way out.

7 Turn the bag the right way out and pull out the lining. Sew up the remaining side by hand, using invisible stitches.

8 If you wish, you can add an imitation-leather loop on the box tape end of the zip and sew it on by hand.

BERBER-INSPIRED RUG

This soft rug takes inspiration from the Barbary coast. The tribes there, of Beni Ouarain, are famous for the quality of their rugs: often known as Berber rugs, they are generally cream-coloured and decorated with stripes or geometric shapes in brown or black. Their neutral colours mean they go well with all styles of interior décor.

TOOLS

1 gymnastic hoop –
I have used a 50cm (20in) diameter hoop, but you could make yours larger if you wish

1 pair of scissors

1 tapestry needle

1 square of anti-slip rug backing, slightly larger than your hoop

FIBRES

1 reel of thick white cotton twine

1 skein of ecru super chunky wool, at least 100m (110yds) in length

1 skein of black super chunky wool

1 ball of black metallic speckled wool

STITCHES USED

basic stitch

braid

lark's head knot

soumak

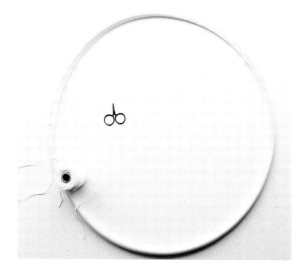

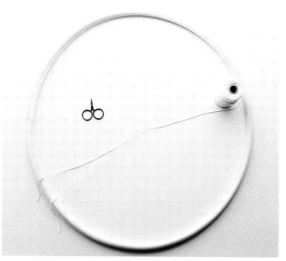

1 String the warp thread by knotting a length of thick cotton twine directly across the hoop. Ensure the ends are tightly knotted so they do not move while you are weaving.

2 Repeat this process all the way around the circumference of the hoop, crossing the warp threads in the centre. I have used seventeen lengths of twine.

3 To get an uneven number of warp threads, begin by knotting one end of your last length of twine to the hoop as before.

4 Knot the other end in the centre of the circle round the other warp threads.

5 Weave the rest of the length of twine around the centre using the basic stitch, to secure the twine. It does not matter where you begin.

6 Your extra-large, circular loom is ready.

7 Cut a long length of ecru super chunky wool and weave a few rows using the basic stitch. A spiral will begin to form and the stitches will automatically weave alternately to the ones in the previous round, due to the uneven number of warp threads.

8 Take a length of black super chunky wool and double it with a length of black speckled metallic wool. Fold it in half and knot it around a warp thread using a lark's head knot.

9 Take the ends and wind them together around the next warp thread, from front to back, to make a braid (see also pages 70 and 71).

10 Complete the braid over a section of the weave and then knot the ends, working in the tails between the loops of the braid. Push together with your fingers.

11 Using a new length of ecru super chunky wool, knot it to an adjacent warp thread at one end of the twinned black wool and weave using the basic stitch.

12 Weave several rounds, and then knot the end to a warp thread between the two previous rounds at the back of the weave.

13 Create a second length of braiding using a length of black super chunky wool doubled with a length of black speckled metallic wool, following the same process in Steps 8–10 (see page 155).

14 Again, weave a few more rounds of basic stitch around the braid with ecru super chunky wool. Squeeze the rounds together regularly with your fingers.

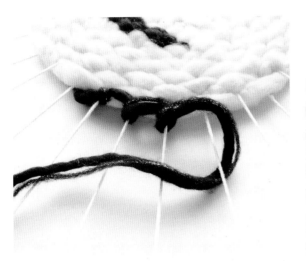

15 To create finer black lines on the rug, follow the soumak technique (see also page 73) using a length of black super chunky wool combined with black speckled metallic yarn. As before, follow these black lines with several rounds of basic stitch using ecru super chunky wool, pushing the rounds together now and then to hold the weave snugly in place.

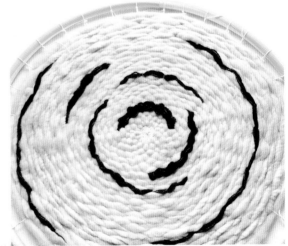

16 Continue to weave the rest of your rug in this way, swapping between rounds of basic stitch using ecru super chunky wool and braids or soumaks of black super chunky wool, doubled with black speckled metallic yarn.

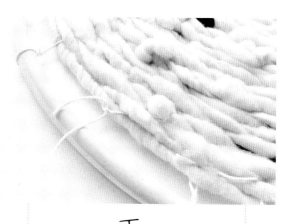

17 Cut the warp threads two by two and use a double knot to tie them in pairs flush against the last round of the weave. The last knot will consist of three warp threads.

Tip

Do not pull the knots too tight as the weave may wrinkle when you take it off the hoop.

18 Remove your weave from the hoop.

Finishing

If you wish, you could stop here and lay your rug wherever you like! However, to give the rug a bit more solidity and ensure that it cannot slide on your floor, I recommend you sew anti-slip rug backing to the reverse side of your weave.

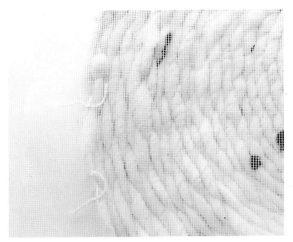

19 Lay the rug face down, wrong side facing up. Take the square of anti-slip backing and place it flat on the back of the weave. Make sure you flatten out any wrinkles.

20 Cut the anti-slip backing to the shape of your rug, making sure that it aligns with the edges of the weave.

21 Thread a tapestry needle with cotton twine and sew on the backing. Begin at the centre, weaving and winding the needle around the warp threads, then add a few stitches at regular intervals throughout the rest of the weave, working your way out to the edges. Ensure that you stitch around the warp threads only.

22 Stitch the very edges of the anti-slip backing to the warp thread knots.

AUTHOR'S THANKS

Special thanks to Barbara, Sylvie and Julie for putting their trust in me, and making a dream come true.

Jeanne and Mark, your reserves of patience, love and support have been my greatest help. The fact that you accepted that I was shut up in my bubble, but remained by my side at all times; your looks, your words, your presence throughout this adventure – all have been most precious to me. You are my reason, my desire, my strength. I love you both.

My mother, who gave me confidence in my moments of doubt, and who reassured me and motivated me throughout my weaving journey: your presence and your words have always been a support to me, and given me the courage to go forwards.

To my father, for being one to forge ahead and challenge me. Thank you for having indirectly passed on this passion to me.

Laura, my sister, I will always remember that afternoon of modelling, and how the house rang with laughter!

My friends, whether you are in Belgium, Japan, England, Québec, Nimes, Bordeaux, Rennes, Paris or in Nantes, close to me. The distance has never made us less close. It was not your passion, or even your interest, but your helpful and motivating words that allowed me to step off the beaten path and walk alone along the road of weaving.

Finally, to the television series whose music that played while I wove: *Doctor Who*!

Publishing management:
Isabelle Jeuge-Maynart and Ghislaine Stora

Editor: Sylvie Cattaneo-Naves

Editorial Coordination: Barbara Janssens

Cover design: Valentine Antenni

Model design and production: Emmanuel Chaspoul

Production: Jenny Vallée

First published in Great Britain in 2019
Search Press Limited
Wellwood, North Farm Road,
Tunbridge Wells, Kent TN2 3DR

Originally published in France in 2017
© Dessain et Tolra/Larousse
21, Rue du Montparnasse, 75006 Paris VIᵉ, France
ISBN: 978-2-29500-690-5

English Translation by Burravoe Translation Services

ISBN: 978-1-78221-701-5

SUPPLIERS
For details of the author's favourite suppliers, please visit the Search Press website:
www.searchpress.com

Printed in China through Asia Pacific Offset